"Lord,

Teach Us

to Pray"

"Lord, Teach Us to Pray"

By Norman Schrock

Rod and Staff Publishers, Inc.
PO Box 3
Crockett, Kentucky 41413
Telephone: 606-522-4348

Copyright 2019

Rod and Staff Publishers, Inc.
Crockett, Kentucky 41413

Printed in USA

ISBN 978-07399-2551-5
Catalog no. 2366

2   3   4   5   6   —   29   28   27   26   25   24   23   22   21   20

Table of Contents

Worship
Incense
Communion
Faith
Communication
Dependence
Refreshment
Being still

Prayer is essential to Christian victory.
God commands us to pray.
Prayer is the gateway to many blessings.
Prayer shields us from the power of the tempter.
Prayer brings us to the throne of God.

"Our Father which art in heaven, Hallowed be thy name."
"Thy kingdom come."
"Thy will be done in earth, as it is in heaven."
"Give us this day our daily bread."
"And forgive us our debts, as we forgive our debtors."
"And lead us not into temptation, but deliver us from evil."
"For thine is the kingdom, and the power, and the glory, for ever. Amen."

Petition
Intercession
Thanksgiving and adoration
Confession and penitence
Commitment

When should we pray?
Where should we pray?
How should we pray?
How long should we pray?
Priorities

Selfish prayers
Prayers of frustration
Controlling prayers
Unanswered prayers
The place of vows

Introduction

Many books have been written on the challenge and blessing of prayer. Yet prayer is a weak spot of many Christians. Thus, we need to be stimulated to practice this blessed gift from God.

F. B. Meyer wrote, "The greatest tragedy in life is not unanswered prayer, but unoffered prayer."

God opened up the way for us to commune with Him through Jesus Christ. He desires to communicate His will and blessing upon us. But this avenue of blessing is underused by many of His children. How this must sadden Him!

Prayer brings growth into a believer's life. The more we practice it, the more we benefit from it and enjoy it. But the less we practice it, the less we feel near to God. And the less victory we will have.

If any one word could describe the enemy to prayer life in this age, it would be *efficiency*. The North American culture has prided itself in being efficient and self-sufficient. Many other cultures have tried to adapt this pattern as well. With technological advances, medical cures, instant communication, ease of travel, and so on, self-reliance tends to replace our need of God. It is easy to put prayer on a back shelf as an emergency tool. When things are going well, we mentally give ourselves a pat on the back and forget God's role in our well-being.

The next greatest enemy is self-love. Ease of life, self-fulfillment, and self-expression are part of that package. God no longer is worshiped, since man worships himself. Of course, this is not a new problem, but it has become more obvious in recent years.

A third great enemy is simple disobedience to the Scriptures. Many people have expressed disappointment about their prayers and put the blame on God. They should have checked their own lives first and compared it with the standard of holiness God has written in His Word.

The aim of this book is to inspire the believer with a renewed interest and zeal to pray to our heavenly Father. Each portion can be read as an aid to one's devotional life, or it can be read as a study book. It does not need to be read in the order in which it is written.

CHAPTER 1

What Is Prayer?

"To define an object is half of its discovery." By defining what prayer is, we may better understand its use and blessing.

We unfold a map to discover new places of interest, and the farther we unfold it, the greater discoveries we find. Prayer, as well, continues to unfold as we define it and use it. God intends it that way. He plans that we understand more of His ways through prayer and communion with Him.

> *Prayer is the soul's sincere desire,*
> *Unuttered or expressed;*
> *The motion of a hidden fire*
> *That trembles in the breast.*

> *Prayer is the burden of a sigh,*
> *The falling of a tear,*
> *The upward glancing of an eye,*
> *When none but God is near.*
>
> *Prayer is the simplest form of speech*
> *That infant lips can try;*
> *Prayer, the sublimest strains that reach*
> *The Majesty on high.*
>
> *Prayer is the contrite sinner's voice,*
> *Returning from his ways,*
> *While angels in their songs rejoice*
> *And say, "Behold! He prays!"*
>
> *Prayer is the Christian's vital breath,*
> *The Christian's native air,*
> *His watchword at the gate of death—*
> *He enters heaven with prayer.*
> *—James Montgomery*

Worship

"O come, let us worship and bow down: let us kneel before the LORD our maker" (Psalm 95:6). The Book of Psalms resonates with worship through prayer. The psalmist speaks of worshiping *"in the beauty of holiness."* As the believer reads these Scriptures, he feels inspired and compelled to worship God along with David and the other writers. That is God-intended!

To worship is to look beyond ourselves and to reach out

to someone greater than ourselves. Every created being has this desire. Within us is a vacuum that we seek to fill with something or someone! If we fail to worship the one true God, we will automatically worship something lesser, perhaps even ourselves.

When the apostle Paul encountered the Athenians on Mars' Hill, he remarked that though they had built many altars, they still had felt the need to build one more altar with the inscription "To the Unknown God." Paul faithfully introduced this true God, who alone could fill the vacuum in their lives (see Acts 17:16–34).

When we worship God, we open ourselves to an infinite, omnipotent, and majestic power, who has no limitations. We are worshiping our Creator, who *"knoweth our frame"* (Psalm 103:14). He knows infinitely better than we do who we are and what our needs are.

As we worship God in prayer, we yield our whole being to Him without reservation. We bow before Him in adoration, praise, and thanksgiving. This kind of praying comes from a true heart that has yielded itself to the will of God.

Jesus told the Samaritan woman at the well in John 4 that *"true worshippers shall worship the Father in spirit and in truth."* This kind of worship involves a person's whole being. It engages his mind in worship as well as his heart and emotions. He worships intelligently and emotionally.

God wants us to have a proper balance in this kind of prayer worship. When our prayers center around our emotions, they center around ourselves. Emotions are a part of worship, but emotions alone are not a safe measure of our relationship with God. Emotions should complement the facts of faith and understanding.

When we remove emotions from our worship and prayer, the result is usually a dry, formal prayer that becomes a liturgy rather than worship. But with the balance that God has designed, prayer worship honors God and brings satisfaction and rest to us.

Incense

Revelation 8:3 says, *"And another angel came and stood at the altar, having a golden censer; and there was given unto him much incense, that he should offer it with the prayers of all saints upon the golden altar which was before the throne."* Revelation 5:8 also talks about the twenty-four elders having *"golden vials full of odours, which are the prayers of saints."*

In the Old Testament, God instructed Moses to build an altar of incense. The high priest then burned incense on it every morning, when he trimmed the lamps, and also every evening, when he lit the lamps. It was a perpetual incense before the Lord (see Exodus 30:1–9). This was a type of the prayers of the saints. David recognized this as he wrote, *"Let my prayer be set forth before thee as incense; and the lifting up of my hands as the evening sacrifice"* (Psalm 141:2).

As our worship and intercessory prayers rise to God, they are like the pleasant, perpetual incense rising in the tabernacle in Moses' day. Prayer lifts the believer's thoughts as he communes and communicates with the Father.

There is one important difference between the Old Testament offering of incense and our New Testament prayers. Today, there is not a moment when we cannot commune with God. We do not need to wait until a certain time of morning or evening to pray. The duties of life need not hinder us in lifting our hearts to God. While doing the laundry, milking the cows, or driving down the road, we can offer the incense of prayer. This is living in the spirit of prayer, which draws God into every aspect of our lives.

The incense of prayer is not only for Sunday. God desires it just as much on Monday through Saturday. Many believers today try to compartmentalize their prayer time and their work time. But true prayer and worship are constant. God is honored when He sees that we make Him our highest priority in our work life as well as in our formal worship times. In that way, our prayers are a perpetual incense!

It is important, however, to set aside certain times of prayer in quiet communion with the Lord of heaven. When we take time each day to kneel before God, we find refreshment, rest, and strength for the duties of life.

Communion

The word *communion* may be thought of as a common union. When we ponder this thought in the light of our relationship with God, we feel exultant, yet humbled. God in His holiness and majesty has designed us to be able to commune with Him. What a tremendous gift!

When God walked with Adam and Eve in the Garden in the cool of the day, they were communing with their Creator. They had a holy reverence and respect for Him. But after they ate of the forbidden tree, their close and free communion with God was ruined.

Each believer who has his sins forgiven and is walking in

obedience to the Bible can have the blessing of communion with God. Living in the spirit of prayer is living in complete yieldedness to God each day. This kind of spirit is always ready to talk with God. It responds in worship, adoration, praise, thanksgiving, intercession, petition, or confession, depending on the need of the moment.

Is this too idealistic? Perhaps from a human perspective, it is. But from God's perspective, He desires that we live in constant communion with Him. And if we fail in our obedience to Him, He has provided for our restoration. *"And if any man sin, we have an advocate with the Father, Jesus Christ the righteous"* (1 John 2:1). Jesus came to restore our broken communion with God. He does so initially at our conversion, and He continues to do so when an act of sin breaks that communion and we repent.

As we commune with God, we are sure that He hears us. Faith is the key ingredient in this. The little boy who is afraid of a loud thunderstorm and runs to his father for protection receives assurance by the sheltering arms of one who is much stronger than he. There are similarities in our communion with God. We have One who is much stronger than we are, and we find rest and assurance as we respond in faith to His care for us.

Prayer is communion because we can open our hearts unreservedly to our heavenly Father. We can freely share with Him the joys and struggles of life. There is no fear of His breaking our confidence or mocking our weaknesses. Communion is the assurance that He understands us much better than we do ourselves, and in spite of that, He still loves us and wishes to commune with us!

Faith

The writer to the Hebrews stated, *"Without faith it is impossible to please [God]"* (Hebrews 11:6). Faith believes that God exists and that He will accomplish His purposes in the earth as well as in heaven. Faith depends on the Power that is higher than ourselves.

Self-sufficient man has no desire to rely on another. In conversations I had with a successful businessman, he kept going back to the fact that he started his business with $20 in his pocket. Today he is worth many thousands more than that. He feels no need of God. He would call himself a self-made man. It is difficult for God to reach such an individual. Prayer is faith when we realize that we in ourselves are nothing. All that we are is what God has done and is doing.

Faith and prayer are inseparable. Through prayer, we acknowledge that we need God. The full-of-faith Christian seeks to know God in a greater way. Prayer is one way to accomplish this. Hebrews 11:6 (mentioned above) further states, *"He that cometh to God must believe that he is, and that he is a rewarder of them that diligently seek him."*

There is a danger of putting faith in faith itself. This is the basis for the "power of positive thinking." This theory teaches that if a person believes in something strongly enough and long enough, it will happen. That is faith in faith, not faith in God. The teachers of the "health and wealth gospel" have fallen for this false teaching. Paul warned against this in 1 Corinthians 2:5: *"That your faith should not stand in the wisdom of men, but in the power of God."* Prayer to God is not a selfish exercise in lifting up ourselves by our own efforts, but it is humbly giving our lives into His direction. We are willing to be used however He sees best.

The exercise of faith as we pray promotes our Christian growth. Exercising faith stretches us spiritually to reach toward God, who is infinitely greater than we are. Our finite minds need that spiritual stretching. It is so easy to be satisfied with earthly goals and values. God wants to lift us up to reach new heights in faith. Prayer is a gift from God to help us attain His desires.

Communication

Friends are friends because they talk to each other and listen to each other. They take time to share their thoughts and concerns. They communicate about similar values and goals. Without this kind of communication, friendships soon end. In fact, we question the sincerity of a friend who has no interest in communication.

According to John 15:14–15, Jesus calls us His friends. This is very humbling, yet it shows His desire toward us. We know that our relationship with Jesus is much deeper than mere friendship. He is our Saviour and Lord; but also, through the intimacy of open communication, He is our Friend.

God has opened the avenue of communication with His people because He desires to communicate with them. First of all, He has given us His Word, which clearly communicates His principles of truth to live by in a very practical way. Second, God has given us the presence of His Holy Spirit, who communicates the will of the Father to us and in return carries the burdens and joys of our hearts to the Father (see Romans 8:26). Third, God communicates to us through fellow believers in the church, who inspire us by their faithfulness. In addition, God has given us the avenue of prayer.

As humans, we usually have three levels of relationships with others. The first level is relationships with those we work with—store clerks, for example— and other casual acquaintances. The second level is with select family members and best friends. The third level, quite often, we reserve all to ourselves. We are blessed when we can let God into that level of relationship and communicate to Him the deepest fears and joys of our hearts. When we try to hide those from Him, we are the ones missing out on a divine friendship. We imitate poor Adam and Eve, who tried to hide from God's eternal presence and knowledge!

In our communication with God through prayer, we must be completely open and sincere, yet in a proper climate of respect and reverence. We address God with words that are suitable to His supremacy and heavenly position. Some people take the thought of friendship with God too far by bringing Him down to their level. Calling Him "Daddy in the sky" or something equally irreverent does not show a proper understanding of how great God is.

The work of Jesus Christ through His death on the cross is our only means of access to the throne. This is a sacred avenue of approach, which we do not take lightly. Jesus is our faithful and merciful High Priest, through whom we find that friendship and open communication with the Father. Jesus is *"touched with the feeling of our infirmities"* (Hebrews 4:15). He was tempted to sin just as we are, yet He never yielded to sin. Because He understands our temptations, we can openly share the deepest feelings and burdens of our hearts. God's mercy is boundless. He rejoices when we communicate with Him our joys and struggles.

Not only does Jesus understand, but He also alleviates our burdens and cares. He has given a clear invitation to all who are heavy-laden. When we come to Him, He will give us rest (see Matthew 11:28). We also have the promise that He will intercede in our behalf as our Mediator (see 1 Timothy 2:5). He is presently at the Father's right hand presenting our daily joys and struggles to the Father. What a blessing!

We also have the presence of the Holy Spirit living within us. He translates to the Father our deep groanings and the inner emotional and spiritual desires that we hardly know how to express. The Holy Spirit understands the language of our hearts.

Too many times, prayer is used only in moments of distress. If we only pray when we come to the end of ourselves, we have yet to learn what daily communication with the Father really is. What poor earthly friends they would be if they only communicated with us when they needed help!

Dependence

A primary Sunday school teacher asked her class, "What would your father do if he had a flat tire out in the middle of nowhere and had no spare tire?" One little boy immediately replied, "He would call up the shop on his cell phone!" That young boy had not learned the lesson of our dependency on God and of the role of prayer in that dependence. Through today's technological advances, we have lost much of our sense of dependence on God.

Satan has tried to substitute many other things for prayer. Technology is just one of them. If Satan can get us to forget our need of God and prayer, he has succeeded in placing a barrier between us and God.

Some people replace prayer with Eastern religious practices, such as yoga, meditation, or hypnosis. Others use sports or good things like music, reading, work, and so on. These all consume time that should be spent in seeking God, or they provide a sense of security that should be found in God. God is intensely interested in communicating with His creation. When we replace that communication with other things, He loses; but we are the greater losers.

Dependence on God requires that we be born again. A genuine new birth will give us a humble attitude about who we are. Our focus will change from the big "I" to who God is and how insignificant we are.

That does not mean we are so little that God cannot use us. He wants to use us, and He will, as we yield ourselves to Him. When we find it difficult to pray because of our reservations about God's response, we need a better sense of who God is.

When we pray to the Father in humility and reverence, our spiritual eyes are opened to His majesty and holiness. Then we respond as Isaiah did: *"Woe is me! for I am undone"* (Isaiah 6:5). God desires to see in us a dependency on Him. He then fills us with His presence and power, and we find the greatest fulfillment in life.

A little boy was trying to lift a heavy object. His father came into the barn and noticed his struggle. He asked his son, "Are you using all your strength?"

The boy replied a bit impatiently, "Of course I am!"

"No, I don't think you are," his father replied. "You have not asked me to help you!"

Refreshment

In some parts of the western United States, much of the countryside is brown and barren. If you fly over these areas on a clear day, you can sometimes see a winding line of greenery that meanders through the brown. Upon looking closer, you find that a river or stream is running through the dry area. The green line consists of trees, bushes, and grass that are growing close to the water source.

This picture draws our minds to Psalm 1, where David wrote, *"And he shall be like a tree planted by the rivers of water, that bringeth forth his fruit in his season; his leaf also shall not wither; and whatsoever he doeth shall prosper."* Psalm 23 draws a similar word picture: *"He maketh me to lie down in green pastures: he leadeth me beside the still waters."*

What are the conditions to experience this kind of refreshment? In Psalm 1, the preceding verse says, *"His delight is in the law of the LORD; and in his law doth he meditate day and night."* And Psalm 23, or the Shepherd Psalm, suggests an intimate relationship with the Chief Shepherd.

These verses do not draw a picture of a dutiful, forced relationship, but one of enjoyment and refreshment. Just as a person can draw a breath of fresh air when he enters the shade of a tree by the river or can enjoy a cool drink of sparkling water on a warm day, so we can experience the refreshment of spiritual shade and water as we draw near to the Shepherd.

Communion with the Father through prayer draws us close to the wellspring of water. We enjoy it. We find strength and courage. We experience the fullness of a Father–son relationship.

If prayer time becomes dutiful, rigid, and formalistic, we are losing out on what God intended for His children. Yes, there is self-discipline involved. Yes, there are "dry" spells in our Christian experience. But they should not be the normal experience. As we conquer those "dry" times, prayer becomes enjoyable!

The wilderness of this world, through which we are walking, dries us up spiritually. We seek for the oasis of refreshment that God has designed for us. Personal prayer time brings us to that oasis; so does collective prayer as a church group. How often have we come away from a devotional time or a worship service and felt invigorated and ready again to face a dry world! That should be a regular experience for God's people!

Being still

In the midst of the whirlwind of life, can we find time to be still? *"Be still, and know that I am God"* (Psalm 46:10). Humans tend to surround themselves with the tangible, the immediate, and the pleasurable. In a whirlwind of activity, only a disciplined mind can become still.

Nebuchadnezzar learned about being still the hard way. His whirlwind of life had been mighty Babylon (see Daniel 4:30). Saul learned about being still on the Damascus road (see Acts 9:3–5). Religious zeal had been his whirlwind. What is yours?

Kingdom building is God's work, not ours, although we are involved in it. God created us to be busy in His kingdom work, not in our own. Yet we know that nearly all of us are involved in meeting our daily needs by some occupation, whether it is housework or a daily job. When our occupation, however, becomes our own little kingdom, we have a problem of not "being still." Our own work creates a restless commotion that takes all our attention.

We need to ask ourselves the following questions as we go through life:

- How can I slow down?
- How can I simplify things?
- How can I bring silence into my life?
- How can I savor this moment?
- How can I shed my protective armor and masks?
- How can I become less demanding in my approach to life?

Answering these questions honestly will help us find rest in our souls and prepare us to hear His voice as we pray.

True praying sets the whirlwind of activity aside while we worship in prayer. Doing this on a consistent basis has a way of reducing the force of the whirlwind. It gets our focus off the tangible values that we easily cater to and places them in God's perspective.

God is interested in busy people. They are often the ones He chooses to be active in His kingdom work. But our enemy gets a foothold when we fail to discern what is most important to our spiritual well-being, amid our schedules, priorities, and goals. When God calls us to do something for Him, nothing else must stand in the way.

What does this have to do with prayer? "Being still" means getting out of the whirlwind of life and stepping into God's holy presence. Prayer time helps us to do that. It stills our hearts and centers our focus on the greater values of life.

> *Lord, I have shut the door;*
>   *Speak now the word*
> *Which, in the din and throng,*
>   *Could not be heard.*
> *Hushed now my inner heart;*
>   *Whisper Thy will*
> *While I have come apart,*
>   *While all is still.*
>   —*William M. Runyan*

Questions for Further Thought

1. Why is prayer such a vital part of worshiping God?
2. What is involved when we worship the Father in spirit?
3. What is involved when we worship the Father in truth?
4. Why is emotion a necessary part of our prayer?
5. Why can emotions become a danger?
6. Why is prayer an incense to God?
7. How has God, who is perfect and holy, made it possible for frail, weak man to communicate with Him in the following ways?

   a. Physically

   b. Emotionally

   c. Spiritually

8. What may be some evidences that we are putting faith in our faith instead of having faith in God?
9. What are some practical guidelines to keep a reverential

fear as we communicate with God and yet to maintain an intimacy with Him as our Father?

10. Why is an independent spirit a barrier to prayer?

11. Why is spiritual refreshment essential to the Christian?

12. How does God teach us to "be still"?

CHAPTER 2

The Necessity of Prayer

Prayer is an essential part of the Christian life. In this chapter, we want to discover why and how the gift and practice of prayer meets our spiritual vacuum.

> What a friend we have in Jesus,
>   All our sins and griefs to bear;
> What a privilege to carry
>   Everything to God in prayer!
> Oh, what peace we often forfeit,
>   Oh, what needless pain we bear,
> All because we do not carry
>   Everything to God in prayer.

Have we trials and temptations?
  Is there trouble anywhere?
We should never be discouraged:
  Take it to the Lord in prayer!
Can we find a friend so faithful,
  Who will all our sorrows share?
Jesus knows our every weakness;
  Take it to the Lord in prayer!

Are we weak and heavy-laden,
  Cumbered with a load of care?
Precious Saviour, still our refuge;
  Take it to the Lord in prayer!
Do thy friends despise, forsake thee?
  Take it to the Lord in prayer!
In His arms He'll take and shield thee;
  Thou wilt find a solace there.
                    —Joseph Scriven

Prayer is essential to Christian victory.

A dear elderly saint was asked, "What would you do if a fierce temptation overtook you?" She replied, "I would lift up my hands to the Lord and say, 'Lord, Your property is in danger. Take care of it quick!' Then I would forget about it until I was tempted again."

Not one Christian can honestly claim that he enjoys living in spiritual defeat. Defeat is darkness, drudgery, and dread. God did not intend for us to live in defeat. He has made many provisions for believers to live in victory. One of these provisions is prayer.

When Satan tempted Jesus in the wilderness, he was trying to defeat Jesus spiritually by reaching Him at the time of His lowest physical strength. We are so thankful for the demonstration of power in Jesus' life during that extreme test. The spiritual strength He derived from communion with the Father rose above any physical weakness. (The account in Matthew 4:1–11 implies that Jesus had been in communion with His Father.)

As we awake to face a new day, it is good to pause and place the day into God's hands. We surrender our wills to His will. Morning prayer is an essential part of our spiritual strength and will help us overcome the potential pitfalls of each day.

Prayer during our personal devotional times and family devotions is a part of that victory as well. When we set these times aside to turn our minds toward truth and God's Word, it helps us sort through the priorities of the day.

Living in the spirit of prayer throughout the day will give us the strength we need in unexpected tests and temptations.

Is there no magical formula or words that we need to recite to attain spiritual protection and victory? The words we say are important, but the meek and humble spirit behind the words is what God is looking for. When the Pharisee prayed in the temple as he did, his words were many. But God could not honor his prayer because of his spirit of pride. The publican prayed a very short and simple prayer. God heard and honored it because of the humble way he prayed (see Luke 18:10–14). So, victory through prayer comes with a humble spirit and an open mind to hear God's voice.

Our heavenly Father cares more than we can ever know

about our spiritual victory. He created us to bring glory to His Name, and He provided a way that we can do that. When we pray to Him, we are giving Him His rightful place in our lives.

God commands us to pray.

Many Bible passages instruct us to pray. Notice the following: *"Seek ye the LORD"* (Isaiah 55:6). *"Men ought always to pray, and not to faint"* (Luke 18:1). *"Continue in prayer, and watch in the same with thanksgiving"* (Colossians 4:2). *"Ask, and it shall be given you; seek, and ye shall find; knock, and it shall be opened unto you"* (Matthew 7:7). Usually when we are commanded to do something, we respond dutifully. But when we obey God's commands, the reward is far greater than any cost. The apostle John tells us in 1 John 5 that God's commandments are not grievous. They are easy to follow and a blessing to exercise. Prayer is an obvious example of this.

Perhaps this is like an earthly parent's relationship with his child. The parent gives direction; and generally, it is in the child's best interests to follow that command. The command is given because the parent loves the child. Likewise, when the child loves the parent, it is easy to obey; and as he obeys, he sees the blessing behind it. Obedience becomes not a duty, but a joy and a reward.

God commands us to pray for several reasons:

- He knows we need to pray for our own spiritual nurture and growth.
- He knows how quickly we tend to depend on our own resources and ways. Prayer is a way of helping us to

see in our own hearts an independent spirit that has not yet understood its utter helplessness outside of God.

- He knows our inner needs and weaknesses and has offered prayer as a way to care for those weaknesses and character flaws.
- He wishes to reveal more of His nature to us through prayer. God intends prayer to be a two-way communication.
- His grace is extended to His people as they pray. As we noted earlier, prayer is incense to God. He favors those who send Him the offering of incense. And He responds by giving them grace, love, and direction for their lives.
- He knows the power of intercessory prayer and that it meets the needs of the eternal kingdom. God is honored when we pray for others' needs.

Forced prayers are not a blessing, but spirit-breathed prayers are a joy to the believer. He treasures his relationship with his Father in heaven.

Prayer is the gateway to many blessings.

In St. Louis, Missouri, stands the giant "Gateway Arch." This representation of the "Gateway to the West" was built to commemorate westward expansion. It is a grand structure, but we could never experience all the beauty and grandeur of the West if we stayed at the arch. It is only the gateway. It signifies that there is more out there to see.

Prayer is like that. When we open our spirits to our heavenly Father in prayer, we invite Him into our lives to bestow on us His grace, His sustenance, His teaching, and His guidance.

Jesus invites us, in John 16:24, to ask so that we might receive and so that our joy might be full. He further explains that when we pray, He will reveal the Father to us plainly. What greater blessing is there than to know our heavenly Father more intimately?

On the road to Emmaus, Jesus revealed the Scriptures to two seeking disciples. Their testimony afterward was, *"Did not our heart burn within us?"* (Luke 24:32). So our hearts will burn with inspiration and zeal when we see the Father more plainly.

In Luke 11:11–12, Jesus gave the example of an earthly father who would never consider giving his son a scorpion instead of an egg, or a stone instead of bread, or a serpent instead of a fish. How much less, Jesus concluded, will the heavenly Father do something damaging when we ask Him for something good! But how many times do we simply stand at the gateway instead of moving into our Father's further delights? Prayer is the gateway to many blessings!

But we must pray! When we do not take time to pray, we lose the good things God has designed for His children. We lose power with Him, peace with Him, victory over evil, and protection from evil. We lose His grace for our needs each day. Prayer-less Christians are powerless Christians—and soon, not Christians at all!

Prayer shields us from the power of the tempter.

We have a spiritual enemy whose goal is to draw the believer away from God. He snatches the good seed away, sows tares among the wheat, and causes men to sin. In addition, our carnal nature wants to revive itself. And we live in a world of great sin and depravity. Do we need strength beyond our own? Yes, indeed!

When Jesus taught us to pray, *"And lead us not into temptation, but deliver us from evil,"* He was not making a casual suggestion. Instead, He gave this directive for our spiritual victory and our protection from temptation. Sometimes we call this protection the fence of God. Job experienced it as a hedge in his day (see Job 1:10). And still today, we can enjoy the marvels of His protection from evil as we yield our lives to Him. That does not mean we will never have trouble, but it does mean that God's grace will always be available to see us through to victory.

A lack of committing ourselves to a daily walk with God in prayer will make a gap in the fence of protection around us. That means the enemy has easier access, and we will find the Christian life to be a struggle. Jesus reminded His disciples, *"Watch and pray, that ye enter not into temptation: the spirit indeed is willing, but the flesh is weak"* (Matthew 26:41). This was just before Jesus' trial and crucifixion. But the disciples did not watch and pray. They were bone-weary and slept while Jesus agonized in prayer. Perhaps if they had prayed instead of sleeping, they may have had the strength to stand by Jesus in His darkest hour. Instead, they fled.

Satan will suggest many excuses when we need to pray. He will whisper, "There is not enough time" or "You're too tired tonight" or "It's too inconvenient right now." When he does so, we must remain committed to pray. Prayer gives us the ability, through God's strength, to stand firm in the most difficult and trying time.

Prayer brings us to the throne of God.

The Scriptures speak of the glory and majesty of the throne of God. Our prayers reach that throne. And the glory of that throne does not diminish the intense interest that our almighty Father has in our joys, intercessions, and difficulties, which we bring to Him.

Prayer lifts us to heavenly realms, which we can enjoy even though we are limited within our physical bodies. Ephesians 2:6 talks about sitting together in heavenly places in Christ Jesus. One aspect of this is our communion with the heavenly Father. Of course, in our future home in heaven, we will realize this communion in its fullness. But while we are here on the earth, God has provided, through His Holy Spirit living within us, that we can express our deep and earnest heart longings to Him.

We worship Him, praise Him, beseech Him, and intercede for others in prayer and communion. And then we intently listen to hear His response. He gives it in various ways. Sometimes the answer comes immediately and distinctly. At other times, it is less clear at the moment; but with time, it becomes clearer. At still other times, we wait . . . , and it seems the answer will never come. But God is always faithful.

Jesus Christ, as our Intercessor at the Father's right hand, stands between us and the Father. Jesus understands our humanity perfectly. Our emotional highs and lows, our desires, and our struggles with carnality are not hidden from Him. He intercedes for us as we pray, and our spirits are lifted from the petty matters of this world and transported to a heavenly realm.

The Old Testament high priests entered into the holiest of holies with much reverence and fear. Today, we also come into God's presence with reverence and godly fear, but with a confidence because of the completed work of Jesus for us (see Hebrews 10:19). Praise His Name!

Questions for Further Thought

1. How does a humble, meek attitude in our prayers tie closely with spiritual victory?

2. If we find ourselves living in defeat, what is the first step toward victory?

3. How does prayer become a fence of protection around the believer?

4. What does the phrase "sit together in heavenly places in Christ Jesus" mean to the believer?

5. How does prayer lift our thoughts from the mundane and earthly to the spiritual and eternal?

Chapter 3

Jesus, Our Example

Jesus was our perfect example in every aspect of the Christian life, and especially so in prayer. His relationship with His Father was intimate. We can see that best by His prayers while He lived on the earth. Some of His prayers were recorded for our learning. By studying His prayers, we learn the principles of prayer and develop a closer, more intimate relationship with the Father in heaven. We also develop a more complete concept of Him and how He desires to work in the life of the believer.

The most common and well-known prayer by Jesus is what we call the Lord's Prayer, as recorded in Matthew 6 and Luke 11. Someone has said that it ought to be called the Disciples' Prayer, because Jesus did not need to pray, *"Forgive us our sins,"* since He never sinned. When the disciples asked Jesus how to pray, He gave them this example.

This prayer is not intended to be used as a charm or to be repeated in every prayer. In verse 9 of Matthew 6, Jesus said, *"After this manner therefore pray ye."* It is a perfect model of what any prayer ought to consist of.

When cold our lips, and far from Thee
Our wandering spirits stray,
And thoughts and lips move heavily,
Lord, teach us how to pray.

We know not how to seek Thy face
Unless Thou lead the way;
We have no words unless Thy grace
Shall teach us how to pray.

Here every thought and fond desire
We on Thine altar lay;
And when our souls have caught Thy fire,
Lord, teach us how to pray.

Lord, teach us how to pray,
Inspire the words we say.
O fill our hearts with warm desire,
And teach us how to pray!
                    —*John S. B. Monsell*

"Our Father which art in heaven, Hallowed be thy name."

Jesus taught us that we should direct our prayers to the heavenly Father. From the Father, all life flows, ebbs, and ends. He is the Source of light, life, and love. When created man prays, he can pray to no one higher than the Father. Nor should he pray to anyone lower. Prayers to "Mary, the mother of God" or to any saint, pope, or priest of the present or past are vain attempts in connecting with God.

Our Father is in heaven. This does not place Him at a disadvantage because He is so far away. He just seems far away to our human minds. Paul told the philosophers in Athens that God is not far from every one of us (see Acts 17:27). By faith we see Him as being close and always attentive. He understands instantly what His children are praying. The Holy Spirit's presence in our lives and the intercession of the Son at God's right hand are more instantaneous than any earthly communication ever invented. In fact, God knows what we will pray before we begin!

Some professing Christians offer prayers that try to bring the Father down to the human level. Jesus correctly established that we are to pray with reverence and godly fear. God is not some buddy in heaven, nor is He some kind grandfather that is always at our beck and call.

Our prayers reflect our concept of God. When we pray, an image of a holy and almighty God ought to be in our minds. Yes, He is also an intimate Father, and His desire is to establish a close relationship with His child (see Romans 8:15). But this intimacy is based on His supremacy and majesty. We will recognize this in a much fuller degree when we reach heaven and fall before His majestic throne in awe and reverence.

Jesus used the word *hallowed* in this phrase. This word means "to set apart or sanctify." Such is God's name and person. We must approach God with this attitude in our hearts.

Self-will and pride must be completely stripped away so that we can properly acknowledge the holiness of God. We learn more about His holiness and majesty as we read His Word and are sensitive to His Spirit's promptings in our lives.

"Thy kingdom come."

What is God's kingdom? Where is God's kingdom? When we ask God's kingdom to come, what do we mean?

John the Baptist came preaching, *"The kingdom of heaven is at hand"* (Matthew 3:2). When Jesus began preaching soon after that, He also said, *"Repent: for the kingdom of heaven is at hand"* (Matthew 4:17). What did they mean?

Their teaching brought an understanding that Jesus represented the kingdom of God. As He taught and lived on this earth, His life revealed the kingdom of God. In many of His parables, He used earthly things to parallel a spiritual lesson, which draws our minds to God's kingdom.

Jesus said later, *"Neither shall they say, Lo here! or, lo there! for, behold, the kingdom of God is within you"* (Luke 17:21). His teachings about the kingdom of God should represent our thought patterns, our lifestyles, and our goals. The apostle Paul later wrote, *"For the kingdom of God is not meat and drink; but righteousness, and peace, and joy in the Holy Ghost"* (Romans 14:17).

From these teachings, we gather that the kingdom of God is already within the believer's life. But because of our carnal nature, human limitations, and weaknesses, we have good reason to pray that God's kingdom would come into our lives. We give God a special invitation to make Himself known to us, not only in Bible knowledge, but also in making that knowledge practical in obedience and holy living. We need to grow in understanding and in holy living as we prepare for the eternal kingdom in heaven. We can sing wholeheartedly,

> *High in the heavens, Thou hast Thy throne;*
> *Thou hast Thy throne within my breast.*
> —Hervey D. Ganse

As that kingdom becomes a part of how we live, think, and plan, we can see in a greater way the broad picture of God's kingdom. While it begins within us, it is also being worked out in the lives of others. In God's eternal plan, He has many things in store for His people. As individuals, we can blend together in a greater plan for the local body of believers, the church.

We can also be a part of an even greater work as we relate to the mission and outreach efforts of the church. We pray that His kingdom would come to others' lives. This expands beyond our immediate range and touches lives in many different places. The call of Acts 1:8 is to promote God's kingdom at home and abroad!

The eternal aspect of God's kingdom is our hope in this present world. God has promised His people an eternal home, where the sorrows and temptations of this life will all be past. We pray that the eternal kingdom will come—the future abode of God's people.

In a real sense, we can have a foretaste of what God plans for His people in eternity when we desire His kingdom to be within us right now!

"Thy will be done in earth, as it is in heaven."

This is actually a continuation of the preceding clause. When we pray that His will be done in the earth, we are asking that His supreme power and holiness be demonstrated in our personal lives and in the lives of His people in all the earth.

We can be assured that God's will is always done in heaven. The one time when Lucifer tried to thwart God's will, heaven was purged of everything that opposed God. Since then, only God's will has been done in heaven.

At times, we wonder whether God's will is being done in the earth. We know that the powers of darkness are working hard to stop His will from being accomplished. And they have turned men's hearts away from repentance to do evil. But we also know that in the end, the will of God will be accomplished. The laws of God do not allow anything else to happen. God has given man the power to choose evil, but not the power to get good results from bad choices! So, finally, man will always bow to the will of God.

Government power is *"in the hand of the Lord, as the rivers of water: he turneth it whithersoever he will"* (Proverbs 21:1). Men often think they have put themselves in power, and we wonder why evil men rule countries of the world. Because of our human limitations, we cannot see the bigger picture as God does. We can understand it a bit better as we study history and see how certain happenings benefited God's kingdom here on the earth. Even then, however, we do not see all things clearly.

The most important aspect of this prayer is letting the Lord accomplish His wishes in our lives, individually. Since our old flesh wants its own way, yielding our wills to God's will must be a daily commitment. If all of God's people would willingly and honestly pray this prayer, many wonderful things could happen here on the earth!

The sincere believer who prays this prayer and follows the leading of God will see a difference in his own life, in his family's life, in his church's activities and worship, and in his community. *"Thy will be done in earth"* begins personally and reaches out to those we interact with.

"Thy will be done in earth" is a form of intercessory prayer as well. We probably underestimate the power of intercession. When we see the struggles, fears, and tests of other individuals, we can pray that God's will would be done in their lives. The apostle Paul was an excellent example of interceding for others. In his letters, we read of his concern and prayers for the saints. Let us be faithful in following his example in our prayer that God's will be done in the earth!

"Give us this day our daily bread."

Most of us have seen the painting of an older man bowing his head in prayer, giving thanks for his bread and drink. His gesture of thanksgiving and petition is appropriate; and it draws our minds to God, who is the Giver of all good gifts.

Our prayers will naturally include petitions for our own needs. God wants us to bring them to Him. This does a number of things for us:

- It helps us realize that we need someone greater than ourselves to supply our daily needs. Man tends to think he can lift himself up by his own bootstraps. So, he walks around all hunched over, trying to pull himself up. At the same time, he is trying to pat himself on the back. What a miserable picture!

- As believers, we realize, first of all, that our salvation comes from God; and secondly, that God wants to be involved in our lives, even in the small details, such as our daily bread. We praise Him for that, and we come to Him with those needs, whether great or small.

- It helps us analyze the difference between our needs and our wants. Man is always reaching for something more than he has. Sorting through our priorities becomes an excellent discipline. Jesus lived as our perfect example and gave us godly principles by which to order our lives. We may need to go back and pray again, *"Thy will be done in earth"!*

- It reminds us of others' needs. When we look up from a well-supplied table, choose from a well-stocked closet, climb into a comfortable vehicle, or go about our plentiful work, our hearts swell with thankfulness—and possibly some twinges of guilt. We must not forget that many do not have it nearly as easy as we do. Praying for our daily bread should remind us of others' needs.

- We realize that we may not always have plenty. God may lead us through trying and sparse times. Thus, our prayer becomes a sense of reliance on Someone greater than ourselves. We trust that He knows best what our needs are, and we commit them to Him.

- We are satisfied with this day's needs being met. To fret and worry about tomorrow and the weeks to come is pointless, for as humans, we have no way of knowing whether tomorrow's needs will be met. Trusting God for today really includes tomorrow, because tomorrow the man of faith will pray the same prayer. Does that mean we do not plan for the future? No! It only means we do not fret about the unknown tomorrow.

- We commit our lives into His care. We believe the Scripture in Matthew 6, where Jesus taught us that if God can take care of the fowls of the air and the lilies and grass of the field, how much more will He take care of us! God knows the number of hairs on our heads, whether thin and graying, or full! He knows when our last breath will be. He knows the choices we will make tomorrow. Surely He sees when we are hungry! His supply may not always be what we would like, but His promise is to provide.

- Praying for our daily bread points us to Jesus as our Living Bread. We come to Him for our spiritual sustenance. So, in praying for our daily bread, we can ask for our spiritual needs to be supplied as well as the physical needs of life. God is intensely interested in both.

"And forgive us our debts, as we forgive our debtors."

Luke wrote it this way: *"And forgive us our sins; for we also forgive every one that is indebted to us"* (Luke 11:4). This aspect of our prayer life is vital to our relationship with God. In one sense, His mercy toward us is measured by our mercy toward others. This is not to say that God's mercy is limited; rather, our actions toward others limit His mercy to us.

Jesus made this very plain by His parable of the unjust

servant in Matthew 18:23–35. The debt someone else owed him (in our money, probably less than a day's wages) did not compare with the millions he owed his lord. Of course, the lesson Jesus wanted to teach was the immensity of our transgression against God in comparison with what others may have done against us. If we cannot forgive those little transgressions, how can we expect God to forgive our great sin against Him?

An unforgiving spirit will lead us farther from God and into other sins. Bitterness, grudges, malice, estrangements, emotional distress, and even physical problems result from an unforgiving spirit. The story of the feud between the Hatfields and the McCoys illustrates the hatred and revenge that can result from unforgiveness. These two families lived in the hills of eastern Kentucky and West Virginia and retaliated back and forth with lawsuits, stealing, murders, and other violence. This feud lasted over several decades, all because the original families were not willing to forgive each other.

An unforgiving heart will keep us from praying as we ought. It is a litmus test we can put to our prayer life when it seems that God is distant or that our prayers are not being answered. Is there someone we are despising? Is there an authority we are not willing to come under? Are we holding a grudge against a brother or sister in the family or in the church? Are we holding a grudge against our marriage partner? Do we refuse to forgive a good friend who has offended us? Are we plotting to get even with someone who cheated us in our business? All these areas affect our prayer life.

The examples of faithful people in the Scriptures as well as many others help us understand the importance of forgiveness.

Jesus: *"Father, forgive them; for they know not what they do"* (Luke 23:34).

Joseph: *"Moreover he kissed all his brethren, and wept upon them: and after that his brethren talked with him"* (Genesis 45:15).

Stephen: *"Lord, lay not this sin to their charge"* (Acts 7:60).

Jacques Dosie, a 15-year-old lad, imprisoned for the Gospel, in Friesland about A.D. 1550: "We would much rather, according to the teachings of the Scriptures, assist . . . our enemies, satisfy them, if they hunger and thirst, with food and drink, and resist them in no wise with revenge or violence" (*Martyrs Mirror*).

An Amish preacher at the funeral of a young schoolgirl, shot at Nickel Mines, Pennsylvania, in 2006: "We must still forgive. There is no question. As Jesus forgives our sins and our mistakes, so we must forgive others. All others" (*The Happening*).

Forgiveness does not come naturally. We need to humbly pray for God's divine help to forgive. His Holy Spirit is faithful in giving us divine love for particular individuals. It may not happen immediately; but with perseverance in prayer, forgiveness will come.

"And lead us not into temptation, but deliver us from evil."

A spiritual battle is raging to conquer our souls. The forces of evil are pitting themselves mightily against God's people. God is well aware of this. And He is not waiting lethargically on the sidelines to see the outcome. Rather,

He is intensely interested in our victory.

God has given us all the resources we need for our victory. One of those resources is prayer. When God hears our appeal for victory over temptation and evil, He is faithful to respond. His forces are far stronger than the forces of evil; and when we appeal to Him for help, Satan is powerless against us at that moment.

But our appeal must be honest. We must be willing to let this old carnal flesh die. If we pray with any reserve in our hearts about avoiding sin, God cannot work as He wishes.

The prayer above is preventive. Our morning prayer should include asking God for spiritual protection for that day. Then when we are faced with the temptation to anger, lust, greed, pride, covetousness, envy, or other damaging thoughts, we will already have taken a step toward victory. This prayer expresses our need for God's help.

This prayer is also for the moment of temptation. Alertness to the enemy is imperative. He is ever ready to feed our carnal nature and destroy a peaceful relationship with God. We cannot avoid temptations, since we live in a sinful world. But as soon as we recognize the moment of temptation, the only path to victory is our immediate appeal to God for His strength and help.

God has promised that for every temptation, there is a way to escape (see 1 Corinthians 10:13). Escape routes are put in place by God, but we must choose them. God wants us to have victory. When we appeal for His help and He senses our sincerity, He will inspire us with the correct escape. This may happen in the blink of an eye, or it may take some time and concentration. Yet in the heat of temptation, prayer links us with God, the Provider of escape routes.

Here are some of these escapes:

- Continuing in prayer
- Singing
- Finding a brother or sister to talk to
- Keeping a memory passage close by to work on
- Finding something to do if the temptation comes at an idle time
- Praying for the individual who causes thoughts of jealousy, envy, covetousness, or irritation
- Praying for an honest evaluation of ourselves when prideful thoughts come
- Channeling our energy into work when we feel angry
- Considering the end result of rebellion
- Memorizing Philippians 4:8 and keeping it close in the moment of temptation

"For thine is the kingdom, and the power, and the glory, for ever. Amen."

The closing line of this model prayer repeats our reverence for the most holy God.

We have prayed that His kingdom come. Of course, the kingdom is already His. It always has been His, it is His presently, and it will always be His. We sometimes struggle to believe that when we see the forces of evil at work in the world today. But by faith we understand that the evil forces will be overthrown by His power.

The power is God's. The original Greek word for *power* (*dunamis*) is the root of our word *dynamite*. We stand back and gasp at the power of dynamite. But consider the awesome power of God in creation, in salvation, in the sustenance of life, in the appropriation of grace, in the ministry of angels, and so on. It is sad when we limit God's power by our unbelief. However, it is not limited in the overall affairs of life; it is limited only in our own lives.

In this life, we can catch only a glimpse of the glory of God. Moses spent forty days and nights with the Lord on Mount Sinai. When he came down from the mount, his face shone so brightly that he had to cover his face with a veil to speak to the Israelites (see Exodus 34:28–33).

The majesty of God's person, the glory of His throne, and the beauty of His surroundings are all pictured briefly in His Word. We anticipate a much fuller view in the life to come.

Questions for Further Thought

1. What are some helps in maintaining a holy reverence for God in our prayers?

2. What did Jesus mean when He said, "Behold, the kingdom of God is within you"?

3. What may be some indicators that our wills are opposing God's will?

4. How can we plan for tomorrow without fretting about tomorrow?

5. Why is the failure to forgive others such a barrier in our prayers?

6. What makes spiritual defeat so dark? What makes spiritual victory so bright?

7. How can we catch a glimpse of God's glory?

CHAPTER 4

Kinds of Prayer

In the Lord's Prayer, Jesus gave us a pattern of the seven different kinds of prayer: petition, intercession, thanksgiving, adoration, confession, penitence, and commitment. In our prayers, we often combine several kinds.

As with all issues of life, a proper balance is both helpful and essential. We want to achieve that balance in our prayer life as well.

Petition

To petition means "to request formally." In the judicial system, lawyers are well acquainted with petitions. Many court cases have been initiated by a submitted petition. Those submitting the petition have a specific need or goal in view.

Similarly, prayers of petition come from believers because of needs or goals. Most likely, this is the kind of prayer that believers use most. (And it is likely the only one used by unbelievers. The only time many of them think about God is when they reach the end of their rope and need something from Him.)

Jesus taught us about this type of prayer when He told us to ask for *"our daily bread."* He also gave us an example of a petition in Matthew 7:9–11 when He illustrated the request of a child asking his father for bread or a fish. Jesus explained that if earthly fathers respond to these requests, how much more will our heavenly Father hear our requests and respond as He sees best.

The believer needs to think clearly about his prayer of petition. At times, we may foolishly ask for a "stone" or a "scorpion," and our Father in heaven sees that we actually need "bread" or a "fish." Since we are limited in our understanding about the present and the past and know nothing about tomorrow, we must ask God to work His will in our requests.

When Jesus taught us to pray according to His will, He meant that we should consider whether our requests are His will. This has a way of tempering our petitions. As we consider how Jesus lived and walked on the earth, it helps us to make godly requests and to pattern our petitions after His walk.

The natural tendency of mankind is to be selfish. Even after the new birth, we have the carnal urge to watch out for our own interests—or our perception of them. Even the most spiritual mind will at times be mistaken about what is for his own good.

God did promise that He would give us whatever we ask for. *"Ask, and it shall be given you."* The reason our requests are not always granted is that we have failed to meet His conditions for praying. What are they?

- We are to pray in Jesus' Name. *"Whatsoever ye shall ask in my name, that will I do, that the Father may be glorified in the Son. If ye shall ask any thing in my name, I will do it"* (John 14:13–14). Praying in Jesus' Name is more than a liturgical exercise or a charmed phrase. It simply means that we are thinking clearly about what we need, and we are humbly submitting our needs in Jesus' Name. Jesus has promised to be our eternal High Priest. He bridges the gap between us and a holy God.

- We are to walk in obedience (see 1 John 3:22). At times, God, in mercy, may answer the prayers of those who are not walking in His will. That is His privilege. But it is quite presumptuous to expect that God will respond to our pleas when we are walking in known disobedience to His Word. We find the greatest blessing when God grants our requests because He loves His obedient children.

- We are to ask in faith (see 1 Timothy 2:8). The call for all men to pray is also a call to do so without doubting. Trusting faith is a living faith. Dead faith prays by rote and ritual. It really does not expect any answers; in fact, it is surprised if the answer comes. This does not mean that every glad surprise indicates that our faith was dead. Sometimes the believers in Acts 12 are criticized for their lack of faith. However, they surely prayed for Peter to remain faithful unto the end. With the heavy guard placed around him, humanly speaking, he could not escape. They had faith in God to keep Peter faithful, but they did not realize that God had other plans. So, living faith is our exercise of commitment to His will. We follow His will in obedience, even though God's response to our prayers may not be exactly what we had envisioned.

- We are to wait quietly while God answers our petitions. The answer may be a yes (either immediate or deferred), a no, or something completely different from what we expect. A believer who was lacking in the virtue of patience asked the Lord for more patience. He expected the answer to be a special strength of quiet fortitude and stillness in the hour of test. Instead, the Lord sent him one trial after another. The believer asked the Lord, "But why all this? I asked for more patience." The Lord responded clearly from the Scriptures, *"We glory in tribulations also: knowing that tribulation worketh patience; and patience, experience; and experience, hope"* (Romans 5:3–4). This was not exactly what the believer had in mind, but the Lord produced the effect He wanted in His child!

Petition prayers are kingdom oriented. We try to determine His will as we pray, and we come to rest in that.

We know it is always His will that another person be saved. So, we can confidently pray the prayer of petition for someone's salvation. We know it is His will that we grow in grace and understanding, so again we can pray confidently. Regarding material needs, guidance for the future, physical healing, and relationships, the issues are not always so clear. We need to wait for those answers. And we need to wait patiently, trying to learn what God wants us to learn in the meantime. God understands our petitions, but He also sees the big picture. So we leave the final answer to Him.

Intercession

To intercede is to plead in behalf of another. It was probably Paul's own initiative to plead Onesimus's case before his former employer, Philemon. He interceded for a brother that needed his help. God has called His people to be intercessors for the needs of others.

Intercessory prayer could be called love on its knees. When we have a burden for another or a desire to see God's richest blessing on another, we can do no better than to intercede for that person on our knees.

It would be interesting to know what happens in the spiritual realm when a saint intercedes for another. It seems that intercessory prayers bind the powers of darkness and strengthen the hands of God's messengers.

Let us consider three examples of intercessory prayer in the Scriptures:

- Abraham, in Genesis 18, pled for the people in Sodom. He began by asking the Lord to save the city if there were fifty righteous people in it. The Lord promised He would. Abraham continued lowering his count until he came to ten righteous people. The Lord promised He would save the city for ten righteous souls. Only four people came out of Sodom, but then Lot's wife was lost when she looked back.

- Moses, in Exodus 32, pled for God's people after they

had made a golden calf and were worshiping it as if it were the god that had brought them out of Egypt. Three thousand men were slain as punishment. On the morrow, Moses prayed further, *"Yet now, if thou wilt forgive their sin—; and if not, blot me, I pray thee, out of thy book which thou hast written."*

- Jesus, in John 17, interceded for His disciples as well as for the church in the future. His prayer welled up from a heart of love for the redeemed. He desired that His people would be kept from evil, would be united as one, and then would be with Him in heaven.

Believers have a godly concern for others. And when we pray for others, we find our own hearts strengthened. Perhaps the issues of life press upon us so heavily that we find it difficult to focus on others' needs. But praying for others usually helps us to see that our needs are less significant than they seemed.

Here are some practical helps in intercessory praying:

- Pray for the need in a clear, succinct way. State clearly what is in focus. There is little value in being vague about the need unless we know very little about the situation.
- Meditate briefly on the need before praying for it. This helps us to pray more effectively.
- Take the prayer requests home from prayer meetings. During the week, continue to pray for those needs.
- Keep yourself informed about the church's mission programs so that you can pray effectively for particular needs. Quite often, needs are revealed in the mission newsletters.

- Do not give up quickly. The powers of darkness keep on working against God's power. But as we continue to pray for others, it makes the way easier for them to understand God's work in their hearts.

God has promised that the Holy Spirit will help us in our prayers (see Romans 8:26). It was also prophesied in Zechariah 12:10 that the Lord would pour out the Spirit of grace and of supplications upon His people. That promise is being fulfilled today! We have a voice that can go directly to God's throne because of His Holy Spirit's presence within us and because of the mighty Intercessor, Jesus Christ, at His right hand.

We may never see the results of some of our prayers. That really is not important. We will have all eternity to find out some of those things. In the meantime, we simply follow God's provisions and directives in our intercession for others.

Thanksgiving and adoration

Thanksgiving and adoration both arise from a similar depth in our spirits. Both expressions recognize Someone who has given us something worth living for. We can be thankful to persons other than God, but we must never worship anyone other than God. Our thankfulness to others can enhance our worship to God because He is the one who enables others to contribute to our lives (see 2 Corinthians 9:11–12).

The Scriptures call us to be thankful in our daily attitudes as well as in our prayers. Colossians 4:2 tells us to *"continue in prayer, and watch in the same with thanksgiving."* The psalmist invites us to *"come before his presence with thanksgiving, and make a joyful noise unto him with psalms*" (Psalm 95:2).

True thankfulness rises from a sense of unworthiness and gratefulness that expresses itself in many ways. It affects our spirits and our emotions and results in joyful living. The only true expressions of thankfulness and worship, however, come from people who have experienced the new birth.

Situations are not always pleasant. How then can we express our thankfulness and adoration to God? He may even seem distant from us! As born-again believers, we can always refresh our lives with the simple truth that God has saved us from a sinful life and eternal destruction. That nugget is a sustaining power in the darkest hour any saint may face. As we latch onto that in faith, slowly within our spirits rise adoration and, eventually, thankfulness.

A man watched his chicken house burn to the ground. He saw his assets and his livelihood disappear before his eyes. Then he lifted his eyes to heaven and cried out, "Thank You, Lord!" Most of us have not yet reached that plane of maturity! But we still can offer the prayer of adoration and thankfulness for His sustaining grace in the hour of need. It takes a heart of faith to see beyond the loss of assets, the loss of a loved one, physical debilitations, church and family struggles, and emotional distresses. We must thank God for who He is at all times.

It is easy to get up and give a loud and fervent testimony of how good God is, when things are going well financially and spiritually. Is God just as good when the opposite is true? From the human perspective, it is harder to see that to be true, but it is true. God is always good! We need to make sure that our thankfulness and adoration are not based on things and feelings but on Biblical truths that sustain us during the loss of earthly things.

Thankful prayers and adoration to God reveal themselves in our relationships with others. Thankfulness and adoration are personal, but their effects reach out to those around us. Our gratitude results in a testimony for the Lord and a willingness to share with others materially, emotionally, and spiritually. Our hearts can hardly contain what we have experienced in our lives. Jeremiah described it like this: *"Then I said, I will not make mention of him, nor speak any more in his name. But his word was in mine heart as a burning fire shut up in my bones, and I was weary with forbearing, and I could not stay"* (Jeremiah 20:9).

Confession and penitence

When people recognize their sinful condition before a perfectly holy and righteous God, the result is a cry of distress. Consider the example that Jesus gave of the publican praying in the temple. *"And the publican, standing afar off, would not lift up so much as his eyes unto heaven, but smote upon his breast, saying, God be merciful to me a sinner"* (Luke 18:13). It was a cry of desperation and penitence. Another example is the apostle Paul when he first met the Lord in a blaze of light. In astonishment and trembling, he cried out, *"Lord, what wilt thou have me to do?"* (Acts 9:6).

The difficulty of the penitent prayer is that it takes humility. The nature we are born with is proud. Realizing our spiritual needs immediately brings a battle. Our flesh resists the need to give up its hold on our spirit, soul, and body. Our mind must reckon with this struggle and choose one way or the other.

Once we come to the knowledge of our need, we have only two choices. Either we continue in the ways of pride and self-will, or we choose the path of humility and repentance. The latter choice leads to the prayer of penitence because we recognize our need of something much greater than ourselves. We may have tried the path to righteousness through the strength of the flesh, but we discovered it did not work.

The prayer of repentance and confession is a natural result of seeing our need. It is a cry of desperation. When the apostle Paul wrote his first letter to the church at Corinth, he called them to repent of their sins. They evidently saw their need and repented, because Paul commended them for their repentance in his second letter. He wrote, *"For godly sorrow worketh repentance to salvation not to be repented of: but the sorrow of the world worketh death. For behold this selfsame thing, that ye sorrowed after a godly sort, what carefulness it wrought in you, yea, what clearing of yourselves, yea, what indignation, yea, what fear, yea, what vehement desire, yea, what zeal, yea, what revenge! In all things ye have approved yourselves to be clear in this matter"* (2 Corinthians 7:10–11).

The prayer of repentance must come from a heart full of sorrow for sin. If we are sorry only because our sin embarrasses us or because we were caught, this prayer will avail us very little. God is able to see clearly through our words. He understands perfectly if our prayer is only a cover-up to save face. God only honors the prayer that brings about a change of life.

This takes a humble heart and a mind that is open to truth and further growth and understanding. It also takes discipline to change our course. This will affect the places we go, the things we read, and the friends we keep. It is wise to seek out the counsel of the Scriptures, to be open to the gentle guiding of the Holy Spirit, and to look to the guidance of mature fellow believers.

True confession and penitence is painful to the flesh, but joyful to the spirit. The prayer of confession and penitence from an honest heart will bear fruit that brings glory to God and rest to man.

Commitment

This prayer can be a special, life-changing one, or it can be a daily one. We could call it the New Covenant equivalent of the Old Covenant vow. It certainly includes the individual's call to a holy and sanctified life. We appeal to God's throne for grace and help to sustain us in the challenges of our commitment to Him.

Commitment to God must be based on the new birth. To call on God in emergencies and then forget Him the rest of the time is foolish. Secular magazines sometimes print stories about persons who called on God when in trouble. Their prayers were answered, but they continued to live in sin. They completely missed the point, for *"the goodness of God leadeth thee to repentance"* (Romans 2:4).

Commitment to God has its roots in the understanding that we owe God our very life, breath, and strength. Since He has done everything for us, we certainly owe Him much more than we can ever give Him in this life.

So our morning prayers should include a prayer of commitment. We offer ourselves to Him to be used in whatever way He sees best. We do not realize what all may occur during the day. But as we walk with God, we realize that His grace is always sufficient to meet every occasion.

The Scriptures express the following thoughts about the prayer of commitment.

- We owe that commitment to God because He has redeemed us. *"Into thine hand I commit my spirit: thou hast redeemed me, O LORD God of truth"* (Psalm 31:5).
- We trust God to guide our way. *"Commit thy way unto the LORD; trust also in him; and he shall bring it to pass"* (Psalm 37:5).
- Seeing our commitment, God guides our works and thoughts. *"Commit thy works unto the LORD, and thy thoughts shall be established"* (Proverbs 16:3).
- As we walk through each day, we do the bidding of God. *"But yield yourselves unto God, as those that are alive from the dead, and your members as instruments of righteousness unto God"* (Romans 6:13).

So the prayer of commitment each day is simply yielding our lives into His service for that day.

There are special times of commitment as well. We highlight these when we observe some of the ordinances of the church. We commit ourselves when we are baptized and received into church fellowship. We do so when we make marriage vows to each other and to God. We do so at the time of an ordination. There may be other times when a commitment is more personal in nature, such as when we are called by the church to a special ministry.

Special times of commitment must always be accompanied with a sense of humility and dependence on the grace of God to sustain us. At times, such calls may appear to be exciting and glamorous. However, we will soon discover that difficulties await us also. So we face each call with the full knowledge that we will not be able to do this in our own strength.

Questions for Further Thought

1. What are some indicators that our prayers may be too self-centered?

2. Why do petition prayers seem to be more frequent than others?

3. What may be some indicators that God's answer is no?

4. What are some helps in accepting a no from God when we wish it would have been a yes?

5. Why does intercessory prayer help to bind the powers of darkness?

6. Is there ever a time when intercessory prayer for another person changes us and not the other person?

7. What are some helps in developing a thankful spirit in times of difficulty?

8. Why does a thankful spirit and adoration for God seem to be synonymous?

9. Why is humility a necessary part of a prayer of commitment?

CHAPTER 5

The Disciplines of Prayer

Prayer is a time of blessing, revival, and sustenance for the believer. But along with that, it takes discipline and work to make it happen. Ideally, the Christian should always carry with him the spirit of prayer. Yet the reality of reckoning with the flesh leads us to look for practical helps in establishing patterns that develop within us the spirit of prayer.

Walking in the spirit of prayer is a growing experience for the believer. In this chapter, we want to look at some practical helps in this important area.

> "Come ye apart!" It is the Lord who calls us;
>   And oh, what tenderness is in His tone!
> He bids us leave the busy world behind us
>   And draw apart awhile with Him alone.

Mid restless crowds with all their noise and tumult,
No rest, no leisure, find our spirits there;
Our vision fails, our sense of life's proportion,
Unless we seek the quiet place of prayer.

Full well He knows—for He Himself hath made us,
Yea, He Himself was human as are we—
How much we need the calm of sweet communion,
New strength to gain for battles yet to be.

He knoweth how for us to have compassion,
Whose feet have journeyed many a weary mile.
Shall we not go in answer to His bidding:
"Come ye yourselves apart and rest awhile"?

And so He calls us into desert places
Where human voices may not drown His own,
There to receive the fuller revelation
He makes to those who wait with Him alone!
—T. O. Chisholm

When should we pray?

God intended prayer in the lives of His children to be a blessing and not a duty or chore. Although our prayer times involve self-discipline, once we focus more on finding time for prayer than on the prayer itself, we need to re-evaluate our relationship with God.

But we do make time for prayer. We all know that we spend time doing what we love. We converse most with those closest to us. We treasure the gifts that are the most valuable. All of these factors play a part in our prayer time. Since we are earthly beings and depend so much on our senses, it is easy to lay aside the matters that require faith. Basically, prayer is an act of faith. We are conversing with Someone we have never seen with our eyes, never touched with our hands, and most likely, never heard with our ears. What does that have to do with prayer time? Everything! Once we are able to sort out the fact that *"the things which are seen are temporal; but the things which are not seen are eternal"* (2 Corinthians 4:18), prayer time will become more important to us.

Now, then, if praying is one of the most important things we can do, and if it is settled that we will take time for it, how much time should that be? Paul wrote to the church in Ephesus, *"Praying always with all prayer and supplication in the Spirit, and watching thereunto with all perseverance and supplication for all saints"* (Ephesians 6:18). He also wrote to the church at Thessalonica to *"pray without ceasing."* What did he mean? If he really meant we are to "pray always" and to "pray without ceasing," then "When should we pray?" is an irrelevant question. There are several better explanations for these verses.

We all know that Paul never meant for us to stay on our knees all the time. Jesus said, *"When ye pray, . . . "* This indicates a special time set aside for prayer. Since we have the presence of the Holy Spirit in our lives, we can pray at any time. But if we do not set aside special prayer times, our prayers gravitate to shallow petitions and thanksgiving when things are going well for us. Our best worship times come when we set aside time to commune with our Father.

It is excellent to use our devotional time as a time of

prayer. With the Scriptures close at hand, we can share with God the things that lie closest to our hearts. Whether that time is in the morning, in the evening, or halfway through the day is really immaterial. What is important is that it happens. That is a part of the discipline of prayer time. If we never set aside a special time to pray, it is easily neglected.

If our devotional time is not in the morning, it is still beneficial to approach God's throne early in the day to ask for His guidance. Even though we may not be fully awake and engaged in life yet, it is a simple matter to thank God for yet another day to serve Him and to ask for His guidance through the day.

The psalmist gives us inspirational thoughts about prayer:

- *"My voice shalt thou hear in the morning, O Lord; in the morning will I direct my prayer unto thee, and will look up"* (Psalm 5:3).
- *"Evening, and morning, and at noon, will I pray, and cry aloud: and he shall hear my voice"* (Psalm 55:17).
- *"When I remember thee upon my bed, and meditate on thee in the night watches"* (Psalm 63:6).

Our special time of prayer should come at a practical time. We have other things to do and other people to work with. If others must often do our chores so that we have time to pray, we should probably rework our schedules.

Fathers, with their responsibility as leaders and providers in their homes, must find a time when they can look to their heavenly Father for spiritual guidance. How difficult to guide those in their care without the resource of prayer! Busy mothers may find that the middle of the day is better for them when the household is quieter. It gives them a perspective of the day's duties, which may not have been revealed in the morning. With their special role as guide for the children in their care, mothers cannot afford to miss the guidance of the loving Father of children.

Young people should work out a prayer time that will suit best for their parents and themselves. With godly parents, this should be easily managed. But when the parents are not Christians, it may be difficult for them to see the need. However, with proper respect shown, usually something can be worked out. If not, it would be wise to seek counsel from other believers close to the family.

This special prayer time should also be when the potential distractions are the fewest. We will never avoid all distractions, but we should find a time when they are at a minimum.

Finally, remember to walk in the spirit of prayer throughout the day. (See Chapter 11.) Our special times of prayer each day prepare us for a prayerful walk. Without setting aside time to pray, we do not have a good foundation for communing with God as we go about life's duties.

Where should we pray?

The Bible gives some thoughts about the place that we set aside for our prayer times. We need privacy for intimacy with the Father. Jesus said, *"Enter into thy closet, and when thou hast shut thy door, pray"* (Matthew 6:6). In our North American culture, we immediately think of the closet as that stuffy little room where all our clothes hang. If we shut the door, it could almost be claustrophobic. In Jesus' day, the "closet" referred to a more spacious and airy room. In our day, we would call it a storeroom—a place that is private and free from distractions.

It is obvious, though, that Jesus Himself did not always use a closet, or storeroom, for His communion with God. Sometimes He prayed on a mountain or in a garden. One time, according to Mark, Jesus went into a solitary place. Only a very few of Jesus' prayer times were recorded, but we learn from His example that the place was not as important as the privacy when He communed with His Father.

The same principle applies for God's children today. Privacy in our prayer times gives us several advantages:

- Freedom from distractions that tend to draw our minds away from worship and prayer.
- Quietness that stimulates intimacy and the privilege to hear His still, small voice speaking to our needs, giving inspiration, encouragement, or exhortation.
- The ability to focus on our relationship with the Father and His blessings.

For most people, it works best to have a devotional or prayer time that is comfortable, but not too comfortable. Do not try praying while relaxing on a bed or in a reclining chair. If a small desk is not available, at least place a chair in a quiet place where you can sit and kneel comfortably.

In a large family with a number of youth, it may be helpful to stagger the devotional times and places to give each one time alone with God. For the most part, prayer time with the heavenly Father is a private experience. A young person may also seek a private place for special needs. Although we can share the blessings of that time with others afterward, we gain the most if we are able to "draw apart."

But then, prayer time does not need to be so private that

others never see us praying. Many a young child has come away with awe and an indelible impression on his mind when he stumbled upon Father kneeling in the haymow or Mother kneeling beside her bed.

Prayer time is a special event of the day. Then we can pour out our hearts in sincere openness before God. We should find a place where we can habitually and freely do so.

How should we pray?

In our prayers, it is very important to keep the character of God in focus. Our prayer time is a worship experience because of who God is. Jesus taught us, in the Lord's Prayer, to approach God with reverence. He deserves that reverence.

The words of our prayers will reflect how we feel about God. Does that mean we should use only "King James English" in our private or public prayers? Not necessarily. If someone feels more comfortable addressing God in that way, it is not wrong, unless it causes his prayers to become stilted or formal. Neither should it keep someone from opening his heart before God, who already knows what our needs are.

When Jesus prayed in the Garden of Gethsemane, He used the terms, *"Abba, Father."* According to Greek and Syriac students, this referred to the Father in a dual way. He is *Father*, one whom we respect as God; but He is also *Abba*, one who shows a father's affection. In Romans 8:15 and Galatians 4:6, we read that the Holy Spirit will guide us in this manner of addressing our Father in prayer.

We gather from this that we must approach God with reverence but also with love and affection. The affection we have for Him, which grows out of all He has done for us and is doing for us, will take the stiffness out of our words.

Jesus did teach us to not follow the example of the heathen in their vain repetitions and superfluous words (see Matthew 6:7). The Pharisees in Jesus' day used long and pretentious public prayers. But Jesus established the importance of a heart relationship with God, which will result in an intimate and sincere prayer.

When we come to God in prayer, we may as well say exactly what is on our minds. He already knows what is there. He understands the human mind because He was the One who created it.

- When the frustrations of life are overwhelming—take them to Him.
- When the doubts of life create uncertainty—take them to Him.
- When the temptation seems more than you can handle—take it to Him.
- When ill will is crowding out your peace—take that to Him.
- When materialism is suffocating your spirit—take it to Him.

God wants to hear what we are struggling with. And He always has the answer for our immediate needs if we are willing and open to listen.

In our intercessory prayers, we should be explicit with our requests. This is more help to us than to God, because He is omniscient; He knows the one we are thinking of. But as we pray about some individual or situation, God often shows us how we can be of use to that person or situation. When we are too vague in our prayers, the answer becomes somewhat vague as well.

How are we to pray? Always with sincerity, with an open heart, with clarity, and with directness. We will find a blessing, and we will honor God as we do so.

How long should we pray?

There is no specific answer because it varies considerably. Jesus condemned the scribes and the Pharisees for their long prayers, because they were praying to be seen. They apparently believed that the longer the prayer, the more righteous it made them. Jesus taught His disciples that it was more important to live a life that pleased God than to put on an outward show.

North Americans want quick and easy solutions. They admire efficient people. But prayer time will not always work like that.

The Scriptures teach perseverance in prayer. That may not always refer to the length of our prayers but to our continuance in prayer. With today's mindset, we tend to quit too quickly. We do not see the forces of evil that are working against the power of God and His holiness. To kneel and pray for "our five minutes" each day may not be effective against such determined enemies.

We see illustrations of this battle in the Scriptures. In Daniel 10, when Daniel was asking for further revelation, the answer was slow to come because the forces of evil were withstanding the messenger. We do not fully understand how Daniel's continuing prayers helped in this battle, but they must have. God was honored by the sincerity of a godly man who continued to pray. Another illustration of this battle between good and evil took place when Michael disputed with Satan over the body of Moses (see Jude 9). As a third illustration, the Book of Revelation speaks of the battle of the dragon against the heavenly hosts.

Often we give up too quickly in our prayers. This is especially true when we are facing a forceful temptation or some need in the life of another or an especially difficult trial. When we are not able to have victory, let us spend more time in prayer. Our enemy does not want us to overcome. When we continue to appeal to God for His help, He will honor that, just as He did for Daniel in his day!

On the other hand, long prayers are not our salvation. God saves us in response to our trust and obedience. We can never cover disobedience by making our prayers longer, as the scribes and Pharisees tried to do in Jesus' day. Obedience and sincere prayers, long or short, honor God.

Priorities

Sorting through what is most important in life is a challenge for everyone. To be a part of God's kingdom creates some potential conflicts in our daily material decisions. Prayer time is a choice we make. At times, it will conflict with our daily responsibilities. How do we resolve those conflicts?

Because we live in the present and are created beings that relate to our natural senses, we tend to place higher value on what is tangible. The tangible is important. In fact, our kingdom loyalty has a lot to do with our choices about the tangible.

On occasion, we will need to alter our normal time of prayer because of material and tangible difficulties. We can hardly avoid that. However, if this happens often and becomes a persistent problem, we have several choices:

- We can continue as we are but eventually realize that our undisciplined prayer time has affected our relationship with the Father.
- We can rearrange the tangible to keep our scheduled prayer time so that it will not be a continual problem. This is the ideal choice because, for some reason, we had established this time as a suitable prayer time. But it is not the only choice.
- We can reschedule our prayer time if the tangible items cannot be changed. The difficulty with this choice is that often some other emergency will come up and replace the one we tried to avoid. This choice is not an unreasonable one, but it needs to be looked at carefully.

Someone may object to scheduled prayer times as too ritualistic and dutiful. However, the unscheduled prayer time has more potential for danger. Prayer will become less important to us if we do not cause it to happen regularly.

Prioritizing prayer as essential for spiritual survival will help to place it on the proper scale of importance. No one does without food unless he or she is on a fast or diet. We know what will happen eventually without food.

Spiritually, we are not designed to do without regular prayer times. If you are struggling continually with victory over sin, spend more time in prayer! Victory is essential to spiritual survival. So we do what we must do to attain spiritual victory.

Questions for Further Thought

1. Praying is a discipline. When does it become a discipline that is not enjoyed?

2. How does a customary practice of certain prayer times help in getting it done?

3. When can those times become dry and without meaning?

4. Why should devotional prayer times be held as privately as possible?

5. What are some helps in keeping our priorities oriented toward God's kingdom?

CHAPTER 6

Problems in Prayer

Since we are human, we will have some difficulties and misconceptions about our prayers. The Scriptures point out these areas. Understanding these weaknesses will help our prayers to be sincere and fervent.

The Scriptures also give a few examples of those who misused prayer. We want to learn from their mistakes.

> *Approach, my soul, the mercy seat,*
> *Where Jesus answers prayer;*
> *There humbly fall before His feet,*
> *For none can perish there.*

> *Thy promise is my only plea,*
> *With this I venture nigh;*
> *Thou callest burdened souls to Thee,*
> *And such, O Lord, am I.*

Bowed down beneath a load of sin,
By Satan sorely pressed,
By wars without, and fears within,
I come to Thee for rest.

Oh, wondrous love! to bleed and die,
To bear the cross and shame,
That guilty sinners, such as I,
Might plead Thy gracious name!
—John Newton

Selfish prayers

Because of our tendency to be selfish, our prayers also tend to be self-centered. The Scriptures have much to say about that danger.

- James 4:1–3 clearly teaches that prayers offered to God for selfish purposes will not be blessed or honored by God.
- In the Old Testament, God reminded His people that when they lived for themselves, He would not answer their prayers or respond to their sacrifices. Selfish living included idol worship, covetousness, and mistreatment of the poor.
- First John 3:22 teaches that when we walk in obedience, God will honor our prayers.

Selfish prayers are revealed in various ways. However, it is difficult to see selfishness in ourselves. We need the searchlight of God's Word and His Spirit to help us understand how selfishness is manifested. Here are a few symptoms:

- When our prayers are mainly focused on ourselves and our needs. Although we do pray for our own needs, we ought to be praying for many other needs as well.
- When our prayer life lacks worship, adoration, and thanksgiving. God is honored and our prayers will be as incense when we praise and worship Him with our words and thoughts.
- When we are taken up with the "health and wealth" gospel. This kind of prayer focuses on good things, like money, goods, and health. God does want to give us good things, but His intent, for the most part, is that those good things be spiritual in nature.

The remedy for praying selfishly is to die to our flesh and crucify the carnal desires that want no difficulties in life. God does not purposefully make our life uncomfortable, but neither is our comfort His goal. The curse of sin brought ill health, loss of money, accidents, and so on. In response to those difficulties, we should pray for God's grace and wisdom to sustain us through them.

Persecution has been the pattern for many Christian believers in the past. In North America, we presently face very little persecution. And that has caused an epidemic of selfish living. We must keep the Scriptural mindset that we are strangers and pilgrims on a journey out of this world. Then, our prayers will tend to be less selfish and more God-honoring.

Prayers of frustration

These prayers are closely tied to selfish prayers but have a different perspective. They are usually born out of an ongoing difficulty or severe test, such as illness, loss, human relationship problems, and church struggles. These prayers lash out at God in frustration.

God understands what we are facing—much better than we do. He will not disregard these prayers, but He does want us to come to Him in calmness and to work through the frustrations without bitter and harsh cries against Him. He is not the cause of our problems; He is the solution! All that befalls us, God has allowed. Prayers of frustration may indicate a failure to believe that God superintends every event of our lives.

Some have said it is wrong to ask God "Why?" That probably depends on how we ask. Let it be asked in the calmness of spirit that still gives God His rightful place as the omniscient One. We may never in this life receive the answer to all the whys of life. We do know, however, that God knows. If He chooses not to answer now, we must rest in that. To ask in frustration will not help us at all. We must repent of that spirit.

Moses' frustration when he struck the rock twice instead of speaking to it kept him out of the Promised Land. God said, *"Because ye believed me not, to sanctify me in the eyes of the children of Israel, therefore ye shall not bring this congregation into the land which I have given them"* (Numbers 20:12). Of course, along with his frustration, Moses disobeyed God's directive. Likewise, when we strike out in frustration against a perceived injustice, we slow the process of God's resolving our difficulty.

Elijah had a great victory at Mount Carmel. But when Jezebel threatened his life, he ran. After a day's journey into the wilderness, he prayed under a juniper tree that God would take his life. It was a prayer of frustration. God needed to reveal the greater picture, and He did so in the next few days. We also become frustrated when we do not see the larger picture. We cry out to God in frustration because from our perspective it looks like things are falling to pieces. God wants us to come back and understand His sovereignty in working out the details of our lives and to also understand that He has a greater plan in store for us.

Frustration often comes when the responsibilities of life become too great for one person to handle. Perhaps it is due to pastoral duties, job responsibilities, household duties, or childcare burdens. The human tendency is to strike out at someone, perhaps even God. And God does understand our frustrations. In those times, we need to listen to His still, small voice. That voice may tell us to delegate some of our responsibilities. It may tell us to back off and try to see God's overall plan. It may tell us to seek counsel from others. It may tell us to lean more heavily on Him and His resources.

God is never frustrated. Therefore, we can come to Him in calmness and know that He has all things under control.

Controlling prayers

These prayers demand things of God. We have a certain perspective of an issue, and we tell God exactly how it needs to be dealt with. This kind of prayer reveals our lack of trust in an omniscient God, who knows infinitely better than we do how to deal with situations.

Jesus was the perfect example of submission when He faced the cross. In the Garden of Gethsemane, Jesus prayed, *"Father, if thou be willing, remove this cup from me: nevertheless not my will, but thine, be done"* (Luke 22:42). As part of the Godhead, He realized what needed to be done; yet His holiness and His flesh shrank from going through with it. But He submitted to His Father's perfect plan and will.

Here are some Scriptures to guide us.

- *"And he that searcheth the hearts knoweth what is the mind of the Spirit, because he maketh intercession for the saints according to the will of God"* (Romans 8:27).
- *"And this is the confidence that we have in him, that, if we ask any thing according to his will, he heareth us"* (1 John 5:14).
- In chapters 14–16 of John, Jesus mentioned several times that when we ask anything in His Name, He will grant our requests.

How do we understand this promise? Does it mean that if we ask anything we wish and make sure to add the words "in Jesus' Name," God is obligated to give us our requests? The obvious answer is no.

Praying in Jesus' Name has an implication that we need to understand. It means that we pray in the character of Jesus. As we study the life, example, and teaching of Jesus, we see His pattern of prayers. His prayers always reflected submission to the Father's will; they reflected His desire to see others helped for the Father's glory, and not His own; and they were always prayed in the context of faith in God's almighty power. Praying in that context is a learning process. We learn it both by experience and by studying the prayers and life of Jesus. We also learn it by faithful obedience to what we know the Scriptures teach.

In its beginning stages, the weaving of a design on cloth, the painting of a canvas, or the design of a building often appears to the uninitiated as a work of confusion. Once the project is complete, however, it turns into a work of function and beauty, and the same observer marvels. There is a distinct parallel between the believer and the amateur observer. God alone knows the beauty of a finished product. We can only see the beginning stages. To us, it may seem that things are not working out and that we need to do something different—pray differently, perhaps! We try to control the situation by manipulative prayer. When God does not respond to this, it is best to rest in the unfolding of His plan!

This brings us to an illustration similar to the one on page 21. In a certain cotton factory, a notice on the wall of the workroom read, "If your threads get tangled, send for the foreman." One day a new worker got her threads tangled. She tried to disentangle them, but she only made them worse. Then she sent for the foreman.

He came and looked. Then he said to her, "You have been doing this yourself?"

"Yes," she replied.

"But why did you not send for me, according to the instructions?"

"I tried to do my best," she replied.

"No, you did not," the foreman said. "Remember that doing your best is sending for me."

Here is where our troubles often lie. We try to untangle and control our "threads" before we call on God!

Unanswered prayers

When we pray and our prayers are not answered, we wonder why. Perhaps there is sin or a lack of faith, or it may not be in the will of the Father.

We prayerfully sing: (and yet we struggle)

> *Teach me to feel that Thou art always nigh;*
> *Teach me the struggles of the soul to bear,*
> *To check the rising doubt, the rebel sigh;*
> *Teach me the patience of unanswered prayer.*
> *—George Croly*

One great challenge lies especially in prayer about health issues. Will prayer change the circumstances in every case? How can one person claim an answer to prayer for a miraculous healing when another, who is also praying, struggles with an ongoing illness? Is it fair that one couple had a seemingly miracle baby, whereas another couple's baby died soon after birth? And both prayed for a healthy child!

Does God override the laws of nature He established at Creation? Yes, He can, and He does so at times. Jesus altered the laws of nature many times by healing the sick, raising the dead to life, curing blindness, curing leprosy, healing cripples, and so on. But we also know that Jesus did not heal all the sick in His region, nor did He make all the blind to see, or raise all the dead back to life. Why not? Why did He alter the laws of nature in one person's life but not in another? Was Jesus unfair?

There will always be unanswered questions because we cannot understand God's ways perfectly. However, can we understand some things about God's methods? Let's notice a few:

- God usually works within the laws of nature, even in the believer's life. Sickness and disease are a reality in this sin-cursed earth. The Christian will just as easily catch a cold or come down with the flu as does the unbeliever. He has the potential to experience the pains of arthritis, the fear of a cancerous tumor, the uncertainty of Parkinson's disease, or the suddenness of a heart attack or stroke, just as the unbeliever does.

- God does honor the laws of nature when a person lives a healthy life by following a good diet, getting proper exercise, observing good work habits, and so on. When such an individual becomes sick, he will find it easier to overcome the sickness than does the one who has violated the laws of nature by overeating, smoking, or taking drugs.

- God does expect that we are willing to use resources He has given by the knowledge of man to restore health. Medicines, herbs, and doctors all have a role in this. When we willingly deprive ourselves of what is available and believe that prayer and faith are all we need for a cure, we are stepping outside His natural laws.

- In every case when Jesus altered the laws of nature, it was for the Father's Name to be glorified. He always pointed men to a greater knowledge of His Father. The healing made them more accountable than they were before. When miracles happen today, the glory must always point to the Father. The charlatans of the faith-healing campaigns will certainly stand accountable someday before God for claiming the glory for themselves.

- In the case of Down syndrome, spina bifida, or other birth disorders, God seldom changes the handicap. He is best glorified when we respond to those situations and are willing to honor His Name through the disorders rather than feeling we have sinned or not had enough faith. To hold out to someone that these situations will be changed if we pray hard enough and have a strong faith is holding out a false and damaging hope. There are laws that God will not change, but He will give us the grace to work with these limitations.

Thus, unanswered prayers are a part of life that will either cause bitterness or bring a continual reliance upon God's strength and grace to see us through.

A doctor who worked in a Swiss sanatorium used to pray, "O God, if this person will glorify You more by being healed, use us here for his healing. O God, if this person will glorify You more by remaining sick, let him be sick."

In the case of unanswered prayers concerning a lost loved one or neighbor, we must also understand the laws of God. We need to persevere in prayer because God will honor the continual prayer-effort for the individual in spiritual need. However, God will never override the free will of man. The person we are praying for will need to respond to God's grace and love just as we needed to. We believe that as we pray, the Holy Spirit is knocking on the individual's heart door. But He will not force that door open.

Unanswered prayers are not because God does not hear His children. While we quietly wait, we listen for what He wants to teach us. The answer may come through miraculous healing, or it may come as added grace to face the difficulty.

Someone said this about "unanswered" prayers:

The Blessing of Unanswered Prayers

I asked God for strength, that I might achieve;
I was made weak, that I might learn humbly to obey.

I asked for health, that I might do greater things;
I was given infirmity, that I might do better things.

I asked for riches, that I might be happy;
I was given poverty, that I might be wise.

I asked for power, that I might have the praise of men;
I was given weakness, that I might feel the need of God.

I asked for all things, that I might enjoy life;
I was given life, that I might enjoy all things.

I got nothing that I had asked for,
But everything that I had hoped for.

Almost despite myself, my unspoken prayers were answered.
I am, among all men, most richly blessed.

—Unknown

The place of vows

We observe in the Old Testament Scriptures that vows were usually made to God through prayer. In the New Testament, the word *vow* is mentioned only two times in the Book of Acts. Both times involved the apostle Paul. He took a vow to please the Jewish believers.

Nowhere, however, do we find instructions in the New Testament for making a vow.

The New Testament church has established at least three vows. The first one is connected with baptism; the baptized one makes a commitment to the church. The second vow, done by choice, involves marriage. This vow commits a person to his or her marriage partner for life. The third vow is made upon the call of the congregation to be an ordained leader of the church. These vows are serious; they need to be taken with forethought as to the consequences and commitments involved.

Should the believer make any other vows? It is difficult to give a definite answer. But the Scriptures do give us some guidelines.

- Our finiteness.

  Jesus clearly told us to avoid the swearing of an oath. He stated, *"Neither shalt thou swear . . . because thou canst not make one hair white or black"* (Matthew 5:36). This cautions us not to make strong statements. We are limited in our understanding, in our capabilities, and in our grasp of eternal values. We cannot predict the future. We really do not know if we will be able to keep the vow in its entirety.

- Our understanding.

  Making a vow may seem like the best for the individual's situation. Even so, it would be better to spend much time in prayer and in studying the Scriptures to try to understand the mind of God in the matter. It is also wise to seek out counsel from other mature believers before making a vow.

It is proper to make commitments to God. Even so, we plead for the grace and strength of God to help us in these matters. When we come to the full understanding of the weakness of our flesh, we find that we have nothing to fall back on as a resource.

Questions for Further Thought

1. How can we learn to live and pray less selfishly by observing the example of Jesus?

2. Will persecution always enhance our prayer life? Why or why not?

3. How does the believer allow difficulties in life to become a frustrating experience?

4. What is the root of our problem when we try to manipulate God through our prayers?

5. How can we best adapt ourselves to difficult situations when God does not alter the law of nature to heal or restore?

6. What are some dangers of making a vow?

7. What are some safeguards in making a vow?

CHAPTER 7

The Intercession
of the Holy Spirit

The Holy Spirit is given to each believer at the time of the new birth. His role in the believer's life is broad and naturally includes his prayer life. Although the Holy Spirit is quite involved in our prayers, He always draws our minds to our eternal High Priest and our Father.

Romans 8:14–16

"For as many as are led by the Spirit of God, they are the sons of God. For ye have not received the spirit of bondage again to fear; but ye have received the Spirit of adoption, whereby we cry, Abba, Father. The Spirit itself beareth

witness with our spirit, that we are the children of God."

These verses give great comfort and inspiration to the believer. This promise has moved him from the realm of the flesh to the eternal kingdom. This is true even while he yet resides in this world and yet reckons with his flesh!

The presence of the Holy Spirit in the believer's life is the fulfillment of Old Testament prophecies such as *"I will put a new spirit within you"* (Ezekiel 11:19). The New Covenant believers are privileged to *"be partakers of the divine nature"* (2 Peter 1:4).

We have also been given access to the throne of God through the work of Jesus Christ, our eternal High Priest. (We do not need to go to an earthly priest.) The presence of His Spirit gives us the privilege to call upon our Father as *"Abba, Father."* This term of affection and reverence appeals to our spirit and soul as we worship Him. (See thoughts on "How should we pray?" page 71.)

The Holy Spirit has been given to inspire, to teach, to comfort, to guide, and to exhort believers to walk in the ways of God. How does that affect our prayers?

- In our communion with God, the Holy Spirit is our Enabler.
- When we are inspired with God's presence, it is because of His Spirit.
- When we are taught of God, it is because of His Spirit.
- When we are comforted, it is the work of His Spirit.
- When we find guidance, it is the work of His Spirit.
- When God exhorts us through His Word and prayer, it is His Spirit.

The Holy Spirit never brings Himself to the forefront.

As Jesus explained in John 16:13, *"He shall not speak of himself; but whatsoever he shall hear, that shall he speak: and he will shew you things to come."* Since His work is in the background, we do not often think of how He is working; but we need to remember that God's way works very well.

Many religious people today talk about how the Spirit has led them to do this or that. This can be true, but we need to be very careful when we say that. Can we say first of all, "The Word of God led me"? If we cannot say that, then we know that it was not God's Spirit that led us to do something. His Spirit will never tell us to do something foreign to the character of God and His Word. Satan, the false spirit, has tried to impersonate the truth ever since he deceived Eve. Something that inspires us in our prayer time or strikes us as true in our walk with God must still align with Bible truth.

When *"the Spirit itself beareth witness with our spirit, that we are the children of God,"* it is because we have been born again and are walking in all the truth we know.

Romans 8:26–27

"Likewise the Spirit also helpeth our infirmities: for we know not what we should pray for as we ought: but the Spirit itself maketh intercession for us with groanings which cannot be uttered. And he that searcheth the hearts knoweth what is the mind of the Spirit, because he maketh intercession for the saints according to the will of God."

These verses carry a promise and give believers a sense of security. We can relate to life's tests and difficulties, knowing that God already understands what we are going through.

He has sent His Spirit into the lives of believers to help us in various ways. But here is one purpose we probably do not appreciate enough: He is not necessarily *the* intercessor, but He is an aid to the Intercessor, Jesus Christ.

That our innermost struggles are communicated to God raises several questions. Let us consider them.

What are these groanings? The word *groaning* is translated from a Greek word that is used only twice in the New Testament. It is taken from a root word that means "to be in straits; to pray inaudibly with a groan, grief, or sigh." It refers to a deep spiritual longing to communicate with God when words cannot express how we really feel.

Is groaning in prayer a common experience for believers? In North America, we are so comfortable that our difficulties are usually surface issues that do not really bring us into the depth of this experience. However, when we lose a loved one in death, or face an especially debilitating and extended illness, or encounter an especially difficult temptation, we may experience groanings.

Perhaps we should sense our need of God more. Has life become too easy for us? Our forefathers who lived in days of severe persecution probably sensed their need of God more often than we do today. We do not pray for persecution; but in these days of relative ease, we must diligently apply our hearts and souls to intimate prayer. After all, we have the freedom to do so!

How are these inner groanings communicated to God? The presence of His Spirit in our lives is the intermediary between our spirits and God, and is the agent through which these groanings are carried to God. We are very thankful that God has provided this outlet for our spiritual and emotional release. We can come to God in utter trust, knowing that He understands the desires of our hearts.

We may not know the depth of our difficulties, but God does. We may not know the answers to our grief, but God does. We may not know how renewal, healing, and strength will come about, but God does. Knowing that God knows is vital to our understanding of the verses above. And in response, we reach out our hands to God by faith and allow Him to guide us one step at a time.

What are the results of this kind of prayer? (Some of them have already been mentioned in the paragraphs above.) According to the latter verses of Romans 8, God is very sure of those who are His. Once we have received the gift of salvation through faith in the shed blood of Jesus Christ and then live in obedience to His Word, we are His. The apostle Paul asked, *"If God be for us, who can be against us?"* The obvious answer is, "No one." Our enemies (the flesh and Satan) continue to work against our spirits. But with all the resources we have, we really have no need to fear or despair. In the innermost groanings of our spirits, the Holy Spirit communicates to the Father our needs. All God asks of us is to reach out in faith for His provisions!

Ephesians 6:18

"Praying always with all prayer and supplication in the Spirit, and watching thereunto with all perseverance and supplication for all saints."

There are four things we especially want to learn from this verse.

In the first place, *"praying . . . in the Spirit"* focuses on the honest sincerity of our prayers. When we pray in the Spirit, we are following the guidelines of the Scriptures for our prayers. After we receive the Holy Spirit in our lives at the new birth, He is interested in drawing us closer to the Father. So, as we communicate with the Father in prayer, the Spirit is intimately interested in this interaction.

The Scriptures speak of the Holy Spirit's involvement in our lives as Comforter, Teacher, Reprover, Fruit Producer, and Giver of gifts. As we pray, He is the one who recognizes the desires of our hearts, and He blesses, encourages, comforts, or reproves according to the need of the moment. If we pray outside of the Father's will, the Holy Spirit is faithful in helping us align our wills with His will. But it takes a sensitive heart to hear His voice. Carnality and selfishness must be crucified, or a hardening process will begin ever so subtly in our hearts.

So, if we wish to pray in the Spirit, we will be very sensitive to His presence and direction in our prayers. We must not allow our own agendas and desires to overrule that Presence in our prayers!

In the second place, notice the terms *prayer* and *supplication*. *Prayer* is a general term. Although we pray on a regular basis, our prayers must not become ritualistic or lifeless. Prayer is the very core of vitality and strength in our relationship with our Father.

Supplication suggests a further urgency in our prayers. We continue to pray until the need is met. Supplication to God indicates an earnest desire for God's will to be accomplished. Although the Holy Spirit is involved in all our prayers, He carries the urgency of our supplications to the Father with utmost speed.

In the third place, we must pray *"always."* In the original writing, the words were written, "in all seasons." Sometimes in the "seasons of life," our emotions take a downward spiral. In those times, we pray. Or sometimes our emotions take an upward spiral. In those times, we learn to temper our emotional highs with Scriptural truths to keep us balanced. Always in our ups and downs, God's Spirit is working with us; always He is consistent. He does not depend on our emotional ups and downs. Let us pray in all the seasons of life!

In the fourth place, we must continue *"watching thereunto with all perseverance and supplication."* It is so easy to give up praying for a need. The word *watch* in Greek means "to be sleepless or awake." It carries the thought of a night watchman on guard against a thief. The prayer warrior is alert to the spiritual dangers surrounding the saints and is diligent in prayer for himself and his fellow travelers. According to *Martyrs Mirror*, James the son of Alpheus had calluses on his knees because of the much time he spent praying. How "soft kneed" are we?

Questions for Further Thought

1. Why can the believer use the term *"Abba, Father"* with confidence?

2. Why does the Holy Spirit never give counsel that is contrary to the Scriptures?

3. How does the Holy Spirit

    a. Comfort the believer?

    b. Exhort the believer?

    c. Guide the believer?

    d. Produce fruit in the believer?

    e. Reprove the believer?

4. How does the Holy Spirit temper our emotional lows and highs?

5. How does the Holy Spirit guide us from immature prayers to more mature prayers?

CHAPTER 8

Effectual, Fervent Prayers

Most Christians wish for a prayer life that is fervent and, as a result, effectual. We can learn principles for such prayers by observing several men in the Bible who were noted for their fervency and effectiveness.

The phrase *"effectual fervent prayer"* is taken from James 5:16. This passage goes on to describe the prayers of Elijah. The original Greek uses the word *energeō,* from which the English word *energy* is taken. It means, "active; mighty; producing results."

This kind of prayer is powerful, not because the person praying is an expert in prayer, but because he or she is righteous. It is not by expertise or professionalism that our prayers become effective and powerful. It is by enjoying a deep, true, and intimate relationship with the Father!

Three Bible men with powerful prayers were Elijah,

Daniel, and Paul. Yet surely, every true saint of God is noted for a fervent prayer life.

> *Lord, what a change within us one short hour*
> *Spent in Thy presence will prevail to make!*
> *What heavy burdens from our bosoms take!*
> *What parched grounds refresh as with a shower!*
>
> *We kneel, and all around us seems to lower;*
> *We rise, and all—the distant and the near—*
> *Stands forth in sunny outline, brave and clear.*
> *We kneel, how weak! We rise, how full of power!*
>
> *Why, therefore, should we do ourselves this wrong,*
> *Or others, that we are not always strong—*
> *That we are ever overborne with care,*
> *That we should ever weak or heartless be,*
> *Anxious or troubled—when with us is prayer,*
> *And joy and strength and courage are with Thee!*
> *—Richard C. Trench*

Elijah

James had just written, *"The effectual fervent prayer of a righteous man availeth much."* It must have drawn his mind to the example of Elijah's life and prayers. Elijah had his ups and downs. His relationship with the Lord had its times of stress. But James described him as a man who prayed earnestly. Let's review some of his prayers.

- In 1 Kings 17:1, Elijah appeared before King Ahab to let him know that there would be no rain until further direction from the Lord. We know that Elijah could not have stopped the rain in his own strength; but because of his close communion with the Lord, he was able to discern God's will.

- In 1 Kings 18:36–38, Elijah asked God to reveal who the true God is. His prayer was immediately answered by fire from heaven, which burned up everything there, including the stones of the altar. That miraculous answer displayed the mighty power of God.

- In 1 Kings 18:42–44, Elijah's prayer was not answered so immediately. He sent his servant seven times before the answer came. Yet Elijah had continued to pray, and James defines that as effectual, fervent praying.

- In 1 Kings 21:17–19, Elijah demonstrated his close communion with God when God sent him to Ahab to show him his evil, selfish ways as well as to tell Ahab his end.

- In 2 Kings 1:15–17, Elijah again demonstrated that he knew the will of God, by taking a message to Ahab's son Ahaziah.

Obviously, the practice of fervent prayer was the warp and woof of Elijah's being. In other words, it was a fiber woven into his entire life. Prayer was more than a ritual. It held meaning for him personally. It was the means by which he revealed the will of God to people. It gave him authority that others respected, and they came to him for wisdom.

Effectual, fervent praying requires communing with God and living in holiness and obedience. This combination is essential in discerning the will of God for our own lives as well as in helping others in their needs.

Daniel

Daniel also was a man of effectual, fervent prayer. His wholehearted commitment is revealed throughout the Book of Daniel as he faced stresses and questions that were thrown at him. From his life, we learn the blessing of fortitude and wisdom that is attained through prayer. Let's notice his recorded prayers.

- Daniel 2:18 simply states that Daniel and his three godly companions asked for God's mercy. There certainly was more to their prayers than that, and God graciously answered that plea for mercy by revealing to them the king's dream as well as its meaning.

- But before Daniel ran out the door with his knowledge, he humbly bowed in thanksgiving to God for meeting their need. This earnest and worshipful prayer is recorded in verses 20–23 of Daniel 2.

- In the next instance (recorded in Daniel 4), when he was asked to interpret a dream for Nebuchadnezzar, it does not seem that Daniel spent additional time praying. But we notice later that it was his custom to pray, and everyone knew it. Daniel had become known by then as a man in whom God resided and who had been given a measure of wisdom seldom found in a man. Later, when Belshazzar requested Daniel to read the writing on the wall, he was ready to answer on the spot.

- In chapter 6, verses 10 and 11, Daniel's commitment in his prayer life is clearly seen. It was so regular that his enemies knew they could count on him to continue his pattern of praying. Daniel knew their plot, but his communion with and worship of his God was far more important to him than the approval of men. So he went right on with his prayer.

- In chapters 7–12, Daniel sought God over and over for wisdom to understand the future events that were revealed to him by dreams and visions.

What can we learn from Daniel's example? Like Elijah, he was consistent in prayer. He did not pray only when he was in dire straits or needed God for a special reason. His prayer time was a tradition that enabled him to help others understand the purpose and will of God, as the occasion demanded. Yet there were also situations when he spent extra time in prayer and fasting as well as asking others to pray with him.

Effectual, fervent prayer seeks God in worship in our prayer times. We establish firmly in our minds who He is, and we earnestly desire to know His will.

Paul

The apostle Paul was a praying man. Throughout his epistles, he expressed his desire for the church and for individuals in the church. Reading through his epistles, one catches a glimpse of the reason for his success in building God's kingdom. He came to God again and again as he faced the challenges of church life, interpersonal relationships, cultural barriers, doctrinal issues, and so on. Let's notice a few of his prayers.

- In Acts 16:25, Paul and Silas prayed and sang praises to God while they sat in the prison. They had been beaten, mocked, and unfairly treated; yet they worshiped in prayer and song.

- Paul's prayer for the Philippian church (see Philippians 1:3–11) reveals his deep burden that the church would grow in spiritual understanding and maturity.

- Paul's prayer for the Colossian believers was similar in content. It is recorded in Colossians 1:9–12. Paul needed to constantly watch out for his own safety; yet he always found time to pray for others' needs. Later, in Colossians 4:2, he instructed them to *"continue in prayer, and watch in the same with thanksgiving."* He wanted them to follow his pattern of prayer.

- Paul often gave thanks to God for the believers. (Notice the opening verses in his epistles.) He appreciated the members of the church and expressed that in thankfulness to God.

- In his letter to Timothy, Paul directed that *"supplications, prayers, intercessions, and giving of thanks, be made for all men; for kings, and for all that are in authority"* (1 Timothy 2:1–2). This was the pattern of Paul's life, and he encouraged others to follow that example.

As New Covenant believers, we have a special privilege to approach the throne of God in our prayers. *"Having therefore, brethren, boldness to enter into the holiest by the blood of Jesus"* (Hebrews 10:19), let us take advantage of this avenue of access and thus experience the fullness of God. *Boldness* in this verse does not mean brashness or lack of reverence, but speaks of confidence. We can enter into communion with God, as Paul did, with the assurance that God is awaiting and desiring our worship and intercession.

Earnest, intercessory prayer for the church in general and for saints in particular is the perfect remedy for difficulties in the churches. Whether it is doctrinal error, brotherhood tiffs, complacency, or worldliness, prayer is the very best foundation for working with any problem. Without it, we will be building on a foundation of shifting sand!

> *When we depend on organizations,*
> *We get what organizations can do.*
> *When we depend on education,*
> *We get what education can do.*
> *When we depend on money,*
> *We get what money can do.*
> *When we depend on fame,*
> *We get what fame can do.*
> *When we depend on man,*
> *We get what man can do.*
> *When we depend on prayer,*
> *We get what God can do!*

Questions for Further Thought

1. What are some requirements for effectual, fervent prayers?

2. How can we be consistent in our prayer time?

3. In Daniel's prayer, we noted the emphasis on worship and adoration. How can we develop this in our prayers?

4. Paul's prayers often included thanksgiving. Why is that important?

5. How does a thankful spirit help us in our worship?

CHAPTER 9

Prayer and Fasting

Fasting has been a practice of Christian people for many centuries. It is connected with prayer and denotes sacrifice for a higher purpose or cause.

For the believer, fasting has deep spiritual and physical meanings that are symbolic of one's commitment to God. It was practiced by Jesus Himself as well as by many others mentioned in the Scriptures. When Jesus taught us about fasting, He did not say, "If ye fast," but rather, *"When ye fast."* He expected believers to understand the need to fast.

Have we lost its value today? Do we know its significance? Is the plentiful food or the soft life or the lack of emphasis on fasting influencing us not to practice it as we ought? Let's consider its relationship to our prayer life and to God.

O God, Thy righteousness we own;
Judgment is at Thy house begun.
 With humble awe, Thy rod we hear,
 And guilty in Thy sight appear.
We cannot in Thy judgment stand,
But sink beneath Thy mighty hand.

Our mouth as in the dust, we lay,
And still for mercy, mercy pray,
 Unworthy to behold Thy face,
 Unfaithful stewards of Thy grace;
Our sin and wickedness we own,
And deeply for acceptance groan.

We have not, Lord, Thy gifts improved,
But basely from Thy statutes roved.
 Yet do not drive us from Thy face—
 A stiff-necked and hardhearted race—
The melting power of love impart;
Soften the marble of our heart.
  —John Wansbrough

What is fasting?

The dictionary describes fasting as the act of abstaining from food or from some foods. The typical dieter understands what that means. But is fasting only a physical discipline? If the goal is losing weight, yes. But for the Christian, fasting has deeper, spiritual implications.

Fasting is not a gimmick to twist God's arm. Someone has said that fasting is designed to change man and not

God. We do not fast to get our own way; instead, it prepares our hearts to understand God's way for us. If something is outside of God's will for our lives, the discipline of fasting will not change that fact, nor will it gain us favor with God.

Fasting often results from sensing a spiritual need within ourselves or in another individual. It may also be for a difficult situation, whether physical, emotional, or financial. The act of abstaining from food helps to bring us in closer contact with the God of heaven. When it is combined with fervent prayer, both body and spirit are brought into subjection. Fasting brings a more intense focus on God and on our relationship with Him.

Fasting also deals with the two barriers that hinder the work of the Holy Spirit in our lives. These barriers are the stubborn self-will of the soul and the insistent, self-gratifying appetites of the body. If we practice fasting as we ought, it will bring both soul and body into subjection to the Holy Spirit's work in us.

Fasting should not be done haphazardly, but with forethought and careful consideration. Perhaps it ought to be considered as one of the ordinances the Scriptures teach. Depriving the body of food has no spiritual merit in itself. If it did, all dieters would be a spiritually blessed people! But fasting has a deeper, spiritual significance of dying to self and of sacrificing willingly for a need.

Fasting is done in several ways:

- An individual fast.

    Jesus gave instructions for an individual fast in Matthew 6:16–18. He said it should be done quietly and without a lot of public attention being drawn to what we are doing. The Father in heaven sees our fasting, and it is His will we are seeking.

- Asking one or more to join in a fast.

  Sometimes we may face a personal struggle, and we may ask others to join us as we seek the grace needed to overcome. Again, this should be done as quietly as possible. The ones we ask may be a spouse, a close friend, or a brother or sister in the church. Ideally, it should be someone we can confide in. They should know why they are fasting so they can pray intelligently for us. Those we ask to join in with us should keep this confidential.

- A collective fast as a church.

  Perhaps there have been divisions and ill will. Calling each member to fast is one way to draw individual minds to a collective spirit of unity if all are open and honest before God. God is then able to speak to the core problem of the difficulty.

  An erring member may be a common concern to all. The call to fast in his or her behalf can be a means of restoring the individual.

  While it may be ideal for all to fast at a given time, it may not always be possible or practical. Some latitude must be given in a collective fast, both for the time and the duration of the fast. God is best honored as each one fasts willingly from the heart.

God has designed that fasting would bring His people into a closer relationship with Him. The physical tends to get in the way. So the need to fast is a part of willing sacrifice, complete devotion, and unflinching openness before God. He earnestly desires to lead His people into greater understanding, greater victory, less worldliness, less worry and fear.

What is the connection between prayer and fasting?

Whereas prayer opens our communion and communication with our heavenly Father, fasting is an added dimension to prayer. For example, when we see the drawing of an object, we can see its width and height. Although we can imagine the third dimension—depth—we cannot fully grasp it until we hold the object in our hand. Then we can experience it. Similarly, fasting adds a further dimension to our communion with God, which benefits the one praying and glorifies the Father.

Fasting and prayer are similar in that both are a path to God. While prayer alone is a discipline and a refreshment, fasting adds the dimension of bodily discipline and self-denial that opens the pathway a little wider.

We can pray without fasting; but we cannot—or at least we should not—fast without praying. That would not be a spiritual effort. A spiritual fast is part of our communion with our heavenly Father.

Fasting can be done merely as a physical discipline, but it will not benefit us spiritually. It is the spiritual dimension and connection with prayer that brings us closer to God and gives us the ability to understand His will in our lives.

What are some guidelines for fasting?

Care needs to be exercised in fasting, in both its spiritual and physical dimensions. The Scriptures give us some guidelines, and there are practical, physical considerations as well.

In Matthew 6, Jesus gave some clear guidance for our fasting.

- It is to be done in private.

  While we may do a collective fast at times, we still do not make it a public show. The Pharisees of Jesus' day wanted others to know they were fasting. To them it was a way of demonstrating their piety. Jesus taught us to appear as usual during a fast.

  Long faces and sour attitudes do not correspond with a spiritual fast. Although a fast is not enjoyable to the physical body and may affect our emotions, we seek to remain cheerful. Jesus clearly taught that a fast does not consist of disfigured faces and sad countenances. The saints of the Old Testament were taught to repent in sackcloth and ashes, and this often accompanied a fast. The New Covenant has changed from an outer emphasis to an inner emphasis. Thus, our fasts are to be done as privately as possible.

  For family mealtimes, some individuals prefer to sit at the table and join in with the typical family time. As one does so, the children hardly notice that one is fasting. Should they notice, not a lot of talk needs to be made about it. A simple explanation is all that is necessary. It should be practiced often enough that it is not a strange practice to the children.

- Proper fasts receive a proper reward.

  When we fast for show, we may get men's praise. But when we do so privately, we receive an eternal reward from our Father, who sees the intent of the heart. Fasting is to be an exercise of the spirit and soul, which affects the body. The body is to be kept in subjection to the spirit and soul. That is a principle that the Pharisees missed, and one that many North

Americans miss for a very different reason. We miss it today because of the convenience of lifestyle and the bountiful supply of food. This has dulled our sense of what we need for our spiritual strength. Not fasting because of this causes us to miss out on intended blessings.

Next, let us consider various types of fasts and their physical limitations.

- Complete abstinence from food.

     This needs to be done with care. Physically, it is unwise to completely abstain from food for longer than three days, without some preparation. Try shorter fasts several times, perhaps for a day and then later for two or three days, before going on a five-day fast or longer. Our bodies are not used to drastic changes; and if we can, we ought to train them beforehand for longer fasts. In the same way, a runner who wants to prepare for a five-mile run usually starts out with shorter distances and gradually builds up for longer ones.

- Abstaining from certain foods.

     North Americans eat a lot of refined-sugar-and-flour foods. Our bodies can handle these in moderation. When seeking God's direction on a less serious matter, a partial fast of avoiding all sugars, sodas, and sweet pastries may be considered. This physical discipline will help us think more clearly in spiritual matters.

     The "Daniel diet" that has been popular in recent years among some Protestants includes only vegetables and no meat. The needed protein found in certain vegetables will sustain the physical body. These fasts can be sustained for longer periods of time.

A combination of complete abstinence for a time followed by a limited diet could be an option.

- Complete abstinence from food and liquids.

    This cannot be done for longer than three days before the body starts shutting down. It is unwise to do this without some preparation. When Moses spent forty days and forty nights neither eating nor drinking, he was kept alive by supernatural means (see Exodus 34:28).

Fasting is not a ritual. Neither is it to be competitive. God designed it for our personal spiritual benefit. Although the method of fasting is important, the spirit behind the fast is what God is looking for.

We read in Isaiah 58 that the Israelites fasted for wrong reasons, and God chided them for it. God wants our fastings to be for our spiritual benefit and not for our selfish pursuits.

Questions for Further Thought

1. Why is it difficult to separate fasting from prayer?

2. When should the believer fast?

3. God chided His people (in Isaiah 58) on their method of fasting. What parallels might there be for us today in our fastings?

4. Why should a fast be done without show?

5. What are some physical limitations that may determine the length and type of a fast?

6. What is the goal of a fast?

CHAPTER 10

Praying Publicly

Public prayers have long been a practice of God's people. Praying aloud draws men's minds toward God in collective worship.

In chapter 3, we looked at the Lord's Prayer (or perhaps the Disciples' Prayer) and considered this model prayer Jesus gave. We do well to follow the same pattern in our public prayers.

> *Where two or three, with sweet accord,*
> *Obedient to their sovereign Lord,*
> *Meet to recount His acts of grace*
> *And offer solemn prayer and praise,*

"There", says the Saviour, "will I be,
Amid this little company,
To them unveil My smiling face
And shed My glories round the place."

We meet at Thy command, dear Lord,
Relying on Thy faithful Word.
Now send Thy Spirit from above;
Now fill our hearts with heavenly love.
—Samuel Stennett

Leading in worship

When called upon to lead in public prayer, we should undertake it with care. Public prayers are designed to lead the group in worship. Just as a person prepares to share in public teaching, so also, one needs to think about praying publicly so that all will benefit.

Some church groups use prayer books. They have certain prayers to pray on certain occasions. This can be effective, although it tends to degenerate into a form rather than being a true expression from the heart. Memorizing a prayer may not be a good answer either.

However, we can learn something about propriety in prayer from the form. We avoid praying according to ritual, but we do pray appropriately for the occasion.

Keeping in mind some basic principles will help to make our prayers effective in public worship.

- Prayer is worship.

    The one who leads out in public prayer is leading others in their worship of God. As in personal, private prayer, the focus of the prayer is communication with God.

A personal sense of reverence and godly fear will produce a worshipful prayer. If the one praying publicly does not have an intimate, personal relationship with God, it will be difficult to convey that through a public prayer. Some have learned by rote what to say and how to say it. Such a prayer may sound right, yet fail to inspire worship in the ones being led in prayer.

- It is directed to God.

Public prayer should not be used to teach others about our understanding of the Scriptures. Neither should it be used to reprimand someone publicly.

When praying publicly, think of Jesus Christ, who is seated at the right hand of God. Jesus is the pathway to God and is interceding in our behalf. Therefore, we humbly pray.

- We must see ourselves as we are.

Praying eloquently may impress people, but it will never impress God. Jesus gave some of His sharpest criticism to the Pharisees, who stood on the street corners and made eloquent, self-exalting prayers. Effective public praying avoids that.

Dropping our voices an octave lower and becoming wordier than normal can be an attempt to impress people. (No doubt, some people alter their tones and terms out of a sense of awe before God, and we should not judge them for that.)

Understanding where we would be without God brings humility into our prayers and makes them effective both with God and man.

- We pray according to the occasion.

    Are we offering an opening prayer, a closing prayer, or a prayer before Sunday school? A prayer at a funeral will be different in content and emotion from a prayer at a wedding. A prayer at an ordination service will be different from one at a hymn sing. The prayer should draw everyone's minds toward the purpose of the occasion and lead everyone into a sense of reverence for God.

Public prayer is an important part of our collective worship. Some forethought and preparation should be given to that part of the service, just as we would prepare for a devotional. To be asked to pray spontaneously need not be awkward for us if we have prepared ourselves ahead of time. Above all, we should be cultivating meaningful private prayers so that we are in touch with God. Then we can lead out with humility and joyful confidence as we worship God and petition Him through prayer!

Reverence in language

Reverence is conveyed not only by the spirit of the prayer but also by the words we say as well as how we say them. In these days of casual Christianity, we should be careful to pray in such a way that does not degrade our high and holy God! Keeping a few points in mind will help others follow along when we lead out in prayer.

- Speak loudly enough to be heard.

    When we kneel for prayer in church, this can become a problem. When facing the back of a bench and praying, raise your head so that your voice carries out over the back of the bench. Otherwise, it will tend to echo back to you, and only those on your bench will hear clearly.

Measure the loudness of your voice by the size of the group in which you are praying. You do not need to pray nearly as loudly in a group of fifty people as you do in a group of three hundred people.

• Enunciate words as clearly as possible.

Sometimes in a larger group, we become self-conscious and tend to mumble our words or to pray too rapidly. This is natural, but a tendency we should overcome.

Take a deep breath to calm your spirit and to focus on God, the object of your prayer. Then speak slowly in order to control your thoughts.

• How formal should our words be?

Because our communication is with a holy, majestic God, we should exercise care how we speak and what words we use. It is completely irreverent to address God as anything less than He is.

Should we use the King James English words *Thou, Thee, Thy,* and *Thine*? Or is it all right to just use proper English? This depends a lot on the speaker. Some grew up using the formal words to address God. Others never learned to do so. There are two extremes in this matter.

One extreme is to be so formal with the King James English that our tongues get all twisted up in the *-eth* and *-est* endings of verbs. We can't quite remember how our regular English word should be altered to fit the style of the King James Version. The prayer becomes stilted and difficult to understand.

The other extreme is to be casual and address God just as we would a neighbor next door. Approaching God in that manner demonstrates an irreverence that mars our public prayers.

A balance between the two is appropriate. First of all, use comfortable but respectful language. Slang and colloquial terms should rarely, if ever, be used. Secondly, do not force your way of praying to conform to another's way of praying. Thirdly, remember that sincerity and reverence for God will help convey the right words.

Personally, I believe there is benefit in using *Thou, Thee, Thy,* and *Thine* to address our heavenly Father. But do not let that become the focus of your prayer!

Here's an interesting point. In Spanish-speaking countries, the intimate form of personal pronouns is used when praying to God. It is the same form the speaker uses to address someone dear to him. He does not use in prayer the pronoun he would use to address a government official or a judge. That would be considered cold and distant. Perhaps we can learn something from that cultural practice.

Our midweek meetings vary a bit from church to church; but typically, we gather for prayer. This custom is important, but prayers at these meetings should not become a ritual. Once our prayers become habitual and nothing more, we will miss the blessings of a united effort to worship God through prayer. Then we should evaluate where we have gone wrong and change what needs to be changed. Prayer meetings should be inspirational and soul-reviving for each believer!

Propriety in conduct

This section is for those who are following along with the one who is praying. Public prayer time is sometimes the most irreverent part of a service! We do well to keep it quiet and reverent.

Consider the following points.

- Listen to the one leading out in prayer, and follow along mentally and spiritually. The Holy Spirit will draw your mind to aspects of the prayer that you can utter in your own spirit. But do not be so carried away with your own prayer that you miss the emphasis of the one leading out. The confusing tradition of some churches where everyone prays aloud simultaneously leads to more distraction than worship.

- Public prayer time is not the time to blow your nose, clear your throat, or get ready for your next devotional. Collective prayer is a united effort to bring our minds to God.

- This is also not the time to discipline your child. Leave the auditorium so that others' worship will not be interrupted.

- Most importantly, this is not the time to write notes, whisper, or cause others to be distracted from their worship. Not only are you hindering others, you too are losing the benefit of worship.

- This is not the time to look around to see who those latecomers are or to see if there are any visitors. Neither should you use the time to daydream or to plan your afternoon's activities.

Worship is so important. As we pray collectively, there is great mutual benefit when all join in harmonious prayer to our holy God!

Questions for Further Thought

1. Why are prayers in our worship services so important?
2. How can we avoid praying ostentatiously in public?
3. How can we maintain reverence toward God in our public prayers?
4. What are some helps in being prepared to lead out in prayer, especially when we may be asked to lead spontaneously?
5. How can we make midweek prayer services more meaningful?

   a. Personally

   b. Collectively

CHAPTER 11

"Pray Without Ceasing"

In this last chapter, we want to consider the important command of 1 Thessalonians 5:17, *"Pray without ceasing."* There are two possible applications to this concise, yet meaningful command, and these two applications complement each other. We must understand the one in order to understand the other. We must do the one in order to do the other!

The first is to live in the spirit of prayer. This is partly illustrated by the words, *"Praise waiteth for thee, O God"* (Psalm 65:1). In other words, every time God looks this way, praise is waiting for Him!

The second is to not give up quickly in our praying. We tend to sigh with impatience when the answers we wish for do not come soon. We also tire quickly of worshipful prayer. God is teaching us to persist in prayer.

Christian, walk prayerfully. Oft wilt thou fall
If thou forget on thy Saviour to call;
Safe thou shalt walk through each trial and care
If thou art clad in the armor of prayer.
                                        —Unknown

Living in the spirit of prayer

To *"pray without ceasing"* is to live in the spirit of prayer. Practically, we cannot kneel in prayer all day. Calls to duty come to everyone, whether it is to plow the field, to drive a nail, to clean the house, or to take care of the children. We all are too busy to give our undivided attention to prayer all the time.

Of course, it is appropriate to kneel in prayer at special prayer times, such as our personal devotions, family worship, and church services. But can we pray beyond those special prayer times?

The following verses speak of living each hour of the day in a ready spirit of prayer.

- *"By him therefore let us offer the sacrifice of praise to God continually, that is, the fruit of our lips giving thanks to his name"* (Hebrews 13:15).
- *"Giving thanks always for all things unto God and the Father in the name of our Lord Jesus Christ"* (Ephesians 5:20).
- *"Praying always with all prayer and supplication in the Spirit, and watching thereunto with all perseverance and supplication for all saints"* (Ephesians 6:18).

In summary, "The man who *walks* with God always gets to his destination."

To live in the spirit of prayer is to give constant recognition to the Holy Spirit's presence in our lives. God's Spirit communes with our spirits, and we cry, *"Abba, Father!"* (see Romans 8:15 and Galatians 4:6). His Spirit is with us all the time, not just at specific times of worship. This is one of the greatest blessings of the New Covenant!

But our minds tend to linger on the tangible. As we face the challenges, the trials, and the up-and-down cycles of life, we tend to focus on them. But living in the spirit of prayer allows the Holy Spirit to join us in the challenges of our daily living.

To live in the spirit of prayer is to maintain a close communion with God at all times. As we arise from our morning prayers, we carry the spirit of worship and prayer with us during the day. The prophet Daniel had the tradition of kneeling three times each day to worship God. Although the Scriptures do not specifically say so, no doubt he arose from those prayer times with a spirit of prayer and worship, which he applied to his duties.

How do we live in the spirit of prayer? It is not complicated.

- Remember that God is with us all the time. As we fulfill the duties of the day, we walk as if God were visibly walking with us. Is this too idealistic? Is it too much to ask that we keep this in our minds? No, because it is a reality. Our Lord has said, *"I will never leave thee, nor forsake thee"* (Hebrews 13:5).

- Live with a God consciousness at all times. This does take effort at first. We commit ourselves to that consciousness, for our minds tend to dwell on the tangible.

- Keep in mind that prayer is a form of worship. When we live in the spirit of prayer, we are also walking in the spirit of worship. God has created us with that capacity.

- While doing our duties, we need to think about what

we are doing, or we will make many and foolish mistakes. Developing a God consciousness will make us aware that we are stewards of His. It will bring a carefulness and a diligence to our work.

- In the mundane and boring duties of life, use that time to think of God and heavenly things and to worship Him.

- When facing temptations, focus on the spirit of prayer. God has sent His Spirit into our lives to help us communicate our distresses. So, when temptation comes, immediately cry out to God. Self-discipline has its place in facing temptations, but the true secret behind victory is the sweet communion with the Father by consistently living in the spirit of prayer by the aid of His Holy Spirit.

- Nurture a sense of God's presence on a daily basis. When we begin the Christian life, God gives us His Spirit to live within us and to guide us. But we must be sensitive to His voice. It takes a commitment of our minds, a discipline of our emotions, and a willingness of our spirits to engage ourselves fully in this way of life!

The blessings of living in the spirit of prayer far outweigh its disciplines. Furthermore, the one who does not live in the spirit of prayer is like a person who lives from hand to mouth. Such a person has made no preparations for his future; he only lives for the present and is barely existing. When a major difficulty faces him, he is at a loss as to how to cope with it. He has no reserves to draw from.

To live in the spirit of prayer is to develop reserves to draw from. We are daily laying up a spiritual "storage room." Thus, we will not become spiritually bankrupt!

Don't give up!

"Pray without ceasing" also refers to the importance of unceasing prayer. Prayer is a discipline that can easily be laid aside. Jesus taught us the importance of importunity in prayer (see Luke 11:8). This is not because the Father in heaven is slow to hear, but because we need to pray for our own good.

Importunity in prayer means we do not give up quickly.

- It recognizes our need of faith in God's way and timing.
- It recognizes that we have an enemy who opposes the work of God and tries to hinder our prayers.
- It recognizes that individuals have the freedom of choice and that God will not force them to change.
- It recognizes that praying without ceasing is a command of God to help us stay on target with His goals and purposes for our lives.

Because of our humanity and finite minds, we tend to give up more quickly than we should in our praying. The success of any project, whether material or spiritual, depends much on one's commitment to it. Continuing in prayer for a specific need takes commitment and discipline.

Many times we may wonder if it is really worth it to keep on praying. But how do we measure its worth? Is it by visual results? Is it by goals to be accomplished? Is it by my measurement? Or is it by God's measurement?

These are important questions to answer. So many times, we quit praying for an individual because we simply have not seen any change. Do we need to see that? How do we know that God isn't working in ways that we can't see? God always works with an individual where he is, to bring him to where He wants him. God's method and our method,

God's paths and our paths, are not always aligned because we cannot see the whole picture. (See Isaiah 55:8–11.) Just because we do not see results doesn't mean there aren't any. In faith, we continue to pray that God's will be done in any given situation or in any individual.

Finally, continuing in prayer is important for another reason. It changes us. As we continue to pray and worship God, it deepens our love and devotion to Him. The shallow Christianity of our day is looking for fast, easy, and cheap results. God does not work that way. God is looking for those who with their whole heart are seeking to know Him. He wants to unlock the mysteries of His greatness as we walk with Him!

Continuing in prayer and communion with God will lead us in the right direction. It will keep us close to God, refresh our spirits, and provide edifying answers to our questions. Why, then, would we not persevere!

Questions for Further Thought

1. What are some practical ways to live in the spirit of prayer?

2. How does living in the spirit of prayer prepare us for the unexpected and alarming experiences of life?

3. How are the discipline to pray and the inspiration of prayer compatible?

4. When may we quit praying for a specific need?

5. What are the blessings of daily, intimate communion with our heavenly Father?